D1560375

The Gospel According to the Earth

*Why the Good Book
Is a Green Book*

J. Matthew Sleeth, MD

HarperOne
An Imprint of HarperCollinsPublishers

THE GOSPEL ACCORDING TO THE EARTH: *Why the Good Book Is a Green Book*. Copyright © 2010 by J. Matthew Sleeth. All rights reserved. Printed in the United States of America. No part of this book may be used or reproduced in any manner whatsoever without written permission except in the case of brief quotations embodied in critical articles and reviews. For information address HarperCollins Publishers, 10 East 53rd Street, New York, NY 10022.

HarperCollins books may be purchased for educational, business, or sales promotional use. For information please write: Special Markets Department, HarperCollins Publishers, 10 East 53rd Street, New York, NY 10022.

HarperCollins Web site: http://www.harpercollins.com

HarperCollins®, 🏭®, and HarperOne™
are trademarks of HarperCollins Publishers

FIRST EDITION
Designed by Level C

Library of Congress Cataloging-in-Publication Data
Sleeth, J. Matthew
    The gospel according to the earth : why the Good Book is a green book /
J. Matthew Sleeth. — 1st ed.
        p. cm.
    ISBN 978-0-06-173053-5
    1. Human ecology—Biblical teaching. 2. Human ecology—Religious aspects—Christianity. I. Title.
    BS660.S58   2010
    220.8'3042—dc22   2009036911

10 11 12 13 14 RRD(H) 10 9 8 7 6 5 4 3 2 1

This book is dedicated to my children. Clark, if I were a parent in some part of this world where children have no access to medical care, I would lift my eyes to God and pray for him to send a physician like you. Emma, you are brave, brilliant, pure, and true. There is no one on earth with whom I would rather listen to *The Hills of Home*.

Contents

Introduction   vii

ONE   **Work: The Garden**   1

TWO   **Water: The Flood**   21

THREE   **Hospitality: Abraham and the Angels**   41

FOUR   **Stewardship: Pharaoh's Dream**   57

FIVE   **Work and Rest: Exodus from Slavery**   71

SIX   **Gleaning: Ruth**   87

SEVEN   **God the Creator: Job**   103

EIGHT   **The First Environmental Music: The Psalms**   119

NINE   **Food: Daniel**   137

TEN   **Community: Acts**   153

ELEVEN   **Simplicity and Consumerism: Philippians**   169

TWELVE   **Sacrifice: Colossians**   183

Acknowledgments   199

Scripture Index   200

Subject Index   202

The Log in My Eye
A Journey Begins

Do not judge, so that you may not be judged. For with the judgment you make you will be judged, and the measure you give will be the measure you get. Why do you see the speck in your neighbor's eye, but do not notice the log in your own eye? Or how can you say to your neighbor, "Let me take the speck out of your eye," while the log is in your own eye? You hypocrite, first take the log out of your own eye, and then you will see clearly to take the speck out of your neighbor's eye.

(Matt. 7:1–5)

One Sunday, shortly after I became a Christian, a pastor and I started talking about environmental stewardship. At the end of the conversation, the pastor told me I had a tree-hugger theology. Now, I don't know about you, but I have rarely heard the terms "*tree-hugger*" and "*theology*" used in the same sentence kindly.

His comment made me wonder: was I on sound theological ground? Becoming a Christian had led me to rethink many areas of my life; the books I read, the movies I watched, and the friends I spent time with had all changed. Should I also reconsider my views on the environment?

Fortunately, Christianity is based on a book, the living Scriptures. Unlike politics and culture, this book never changes. It is the rock on which I base my life. When I have questions, the first place I look for answers is the Bible.

So I asked myself, *What, if anything, does the Bible have to say about caring for the earth?* Using an orange pencil (I wish it had been green), I read the Bible from cover to cover, underlining everything that had to do with nature, God's revealing himself through creation, and stewardship of the earth. What I ended up with was an underlined Bible.

It turns out the Bible has a lot to say about what I think is the most important moral and spiritual crisis facing us today. From Genesis to Revelation, the Bible is filled with instructions on how we can demonstrate our love for the Creator by caring for his creation. He wants us to love every sparrow and every tree—just as he does. And he wants us to demonstrate love for our neighbors by sharing his sustaining blessings.

Reading the Bible through a green lens radically changed my life. Eventually, I left a successful career in emergency medicine to work on the greatest global health crisis humanity has ever faced: the health of our planet. My family and I reoriented our life away from material things and toward God.

In this book, I invite you to walk through the Bible alongside me and share my family's spiritual and environmental journey. Although I was an environmentalist before I was a Christian, I did not *act* like one until faith inspired me to significantly scale back my lifestyle. The purpose of this book is to share with you what I learned and, I hope, encourage you to become a better steward of the sustaining gifts that are on loan to all of us. We will not be merely prooftexting specific passages, but rather exploring some of the deepest themes of Scripture—repeating patterns in the Bible that counsel us to lead lives closer to the example set by Jesus. Further, we will be expanding the popularly held notion of "green." Instead of narrowly focusing on how much electricity we use and what cars we drive, we also will unpack how electronic entertainment interferes with our relationship with the Creator, and how living a biblical 24/6 life instead of a worldly 24/7 life can bring us closer to God.

Throughout this scriptural odyssey you will discover, as I did, that the less we fill our homes with material things, the more contented and spirit-filled our lives will become.

How did this scriptural journey begin? For much of my adult life I did not believe in God. I thought that science and rationality were the keys to unlocking the way to happiness. I didn't go to church, own a Bible, or hang out with people of faith. I had been brought up in a Protestant household—but it hadn't taken. Nancy, my wife, was raised in a conservative Jewish home. We met when she was eighteen, and married when she was twenty. Reactions from family and friends convinced us that religion was simply a means for people to justify their own prejudices.

For the next two decades, we pursued the American dream. I had grown up in dairy-farming country and was working as a carpenter when we married. Nancy convinced me to enroll in college, and a few years later I was accepted to medical school. After residency, we moved to a postcard-perfect neighborhood on the New England coast. I was doing something I loved, and I relished the prestige, paycheck, and respect attached to being director of an emergency room and chief of staff of the hospital. I drove a fast car with a teak dashboard, and when I arrived home at the end of a shift, I entered my three-story Greek Revival house with four bathrooms, custom cherry cabinets, and a separate guest suite.

One February, my wife, Nancy, and I and our two children, Clark and Emma, went on vacation to an island off the coast of Florida. The island was warm, beautiful, and quiet. It had no cars and no streetlights. The narrow roads were paved with sand. The children ran round and round during the day, and I made up games to tire them out.

Once the children were tucked into bed, Nancy and I sat out on a balcony facing the water. The stars shone brightly, and a lovely breeze washed in off the Gulf of Mexico. The palm trees rustled. The children slept. In that beguiling, tranquil setting, Nancy asked me a question that was to change my life forever.

"What," she wanted to know, "is the biggest problem facing the world today?"

There is no shortage of problems in the world: hunger, war, poverty, prejudice, greed, and weapons of every sort. Yet, after thinking for a minute, I answered, "The world is dying."

I gave this answer not because I was a biologist or ecologist, but simply based on my observations. There are no more elm trees on Elm Street, no more chestnuts on Chestnut Lane, no caribou in Caribou, Maine, and no more blue pike in the Great Lakes. This fish is not a rare or exotic species that has fallen prey to extinction. A few decades ago, the blue pike was the most numerous and commercially harvested freshwater fish in the world—thought to be inexhaustible. It was fished to extinction by 1983.

The fields and fence rows in which I came of age have been bulldozed, plowed, and planted with houses. Many people like me have returned to the places of our youth only to find that they have vanished. When Nancy and I tried to find the ford where I had proposed to her, we could not even find the stream. It had been buried under a subdivision.

Similar changes have occurred in humans. We get more cancers, more autoimmune diseases, and more asthma than ever. Our response has been to build bigger hospitals and develop more medicines and radiation treatments. Healthcare becomes more expensive every year, yet we do not ask the question, "Is it because our environment is making us sick?"

Despite these warning signs, our houses, roads, and cities continue to grow. Plans for the future are based upon infinite growth. Yet we live in a finite world. No one should suppose that these trends can continue unaltered for another hundred years and that everything will turn out all right.

We sat there in the tropical quiet for a while. And then Nancy asked a much more difficult question, "What are you going to do about it?"

I did not know, but I told Nancy I would get back to her. When we returned home, I resumed my life as a doctor. On the surface it appeared the same—yet I was disquieted. How does one grapple with a dying world? I had seen and dealt with death both personally and in my role as a physician. But how does one get one's mind around the death of an entire planet?

Around this same time, I came face-to-face with pain and evil. In one week's time, three women were admitted through the emergency room: all three had breast cancer, all three were in their thirties, and all three died. One of the women died seizing right there in the ER, and I had to tell her young husband and two small children that Mom was gone. Not long before, Nancy's brother had drowned in front of our children. And a mentally ill patient I had treated several times in the emergency room began to stalk me. I had all the accomplishments and wealth that were supposed to make me happy, but my life felt barren. I had no spiritual compass to direct me through murky waters.

We live in a world of measurements, and yet the evil and pain I was experiencing could not be measured. Our ability to quantify the things around us has allowed society to realize technological marvels. We find much power—even a kind of comfort and safety—in being able to measure something. Yet, there is a pitfall in our reliance on the quantifiable. If we can't measure phenomena, we may choose to ignore or, even worse, deny that they exist. Evil—like love, hope, and even God—is something that cannot be measured using a double-blind study. Pain and evil defy the quantification tools of modern science.

I began to look in new places for answers. I read through some of the sacred texts of the world. I read the Ramayana, the Bhagavad-Gita, and the Koran. They contain many truths. But I did not find the answer I sought: "How do we save a world that's dying?"

One afternoon I walked into a hospital patient lounge. I sat on a couch next to a coffee table. The table was strewn with issues of

People, National Geographic, and *Time* magazines. On one corner, I
saw an orange Gideon's Bible. I took it home and read it. In its pages,
I discovered the truth I had been seeking. I became a believer—a
follower of Jesus.

What I found in the Gospels is a theology vastly different from the
secular humanist's gospel that I had adopted. Before, I assumed that
science or business or government would provide the answers. Once I
read the Gospels, I realized my heart needed to change before I could
make significant changes—changes that would require sacrifice.

I believe that the Bible provides answers to the problems of every
age. If the world is dying, God has something to say about it. Even
more, he has something he wants us to *do.* Our proper course of
action is woven into the very fabric of the Bible. What we are supposed to do is not so simple that it can be spray-painted on a plac-
ard. Our moral responsibility to God, the earth, our neighbors, and
the future cannot be discharged by simply voting for the right party
or voicing the right opinions. Nor can we rely on others to do the
work of change for us.

Instead, the Bible required me to look in the mirror. One passage
in particular had a profound effect on me. Matthew 7 said that I was
not to worry about the speck in my neighbor's eye until I removed the
plank from my own eye. Jesus, whom I now sought as my guide, told
me that I was supposed to be meek, humble, compassionate, thankful,
forgiving, and—most of all—*cloaked in love* (Col. 3:14). These were
not adjectives that I would use to describe my life. I needed to change.

How could I become more like Jesus—more meek, humble,
compassionate, thankful, forgiving, and loving? Clearly, I needed to
scale back my lifestyle. I needed to focus less on getting, and more
on giving. I needed to consume less, so I could serve more.

Eventually I got back to Nancy with the answer to her second
question: what should we do about the earth dying? I told her that I
would quit my job and start working full time in a job with no title:
green doctor? creation-care minister? ecoevangelist? I didn't even
know how to describe my new calling, but I felt certain that the call

was from God. My decision didn't make any sense in the worldly economy, but it did in God's economy. Although I was leaving the safety of a paycheck, I was not leaving healthcare. I was simply shifting to healthcare on a global scale, trying to help avert the biggest healthcare crisis our planet has ever witnessed.

The home, car, and job—they are now all gone. Our family moved to a house the exact same size of our old garage—don't feel sorry for us, we had a doctor-sized garage. We reduced our electricity usage, fossil-fuel consumption, and trash production to a small fraction of the national average.

This book shares what motivated these changes—the living Word of the Bible—and what I learned: that the Bible holds eternal answers to today's problems. In its pages, I found that God not only loves me but that he loves the tree outside my window and all the birds, squirrels, and insects that dwell in its branches.

What this book does not do is prooftext specific creation-care passages. Readers can easily find a number of articles and treatises that build a strong theological case for seeing "green" as consistent with being Christian. One wonderfully useful resource is *The Green Bible*, the companion book that inspired this volume.

While such books are extremely important, this book is different. In it, we will look at many chapters in the Bible that are not traditionally considered green, and we'll explore how their overarching principles lead to a God-honoring life of stewardship. Instead of just pointing out the most obvious creation-care passages, we will explore pervasive patterns that point us toward a greener, less materialistic life. We will see how using less electricity not only helps us honor the Creator, but teaches us to love our neighbors. We will discuss how remembering the Sabbath is not simply one of Yahweh's top ten commandments, but a counterculture way of life that calls us to *do* less so we can *be* more. We will learn how the principles of stewardship and sacrifice encourage us to choose restraint in a world that says "just do it"—if you can afford it, you deserve it—and while you are at it, have it your way.

I invite you to journey through Scripture with me, visiting some of the most important characters in the Bible and discovering what they can teach us about caring for God's creation through daily spiritual practices. We will allow the Bible to speak for itself and tell us what God thinks of our "all for one and none for all" society, and we will share creation-care wisdom of church leaders through the ages. Once and for all, we will answer, "How would Jesus save the earth?"

I believe that humanity stands at a great crossroads. We hold the fate of God's creation in our hands. This is not because there is no God, or that God is not all-powerful, loving, or in control. Rather, it is the result of our being made in the image of a Creator God. We are free to choose life or death, light or darkness, and the very fate of our own souls. With this awesome responsibility comes not only the stewardship of the natural world we inhabit but the fate of our children, and our children's children.

Today, I understand that God used my tree-hugger discussion with the pastor and a couple of profound questions from my wife to lead me on an environmental and spiritual journey through the Bible. In addition to forcing me to look in the mirror and change my environmental footprint, Matthew 7 inspired me to continue seeking answers: *"Ask, and it will be given you; search, and you will find; knock, and the door will be opened for you. For everyone who asks receives, and everyone who searches finds, and for everyone who knocks, the door will be opened"* (Matt. 7:7–8).

It is my prayer that you will continue the journey with me. Together we will discover why the Good Book is, indeed, a green book.

We'll begin where it all started, in Genesis, the creation of heaven and earth.

Work
The Garden

The Lord God planted a garden in Eden, in the east; and there
he put the man whom he had formed. Out of the ground the
Lord God made to grow every tree that is pleasant to the sight
and good for food, the tree of life also in the midst of the
garden, and the tree of the knowledge of good and evil. . . .
The Lord God took the man and put him in the garden of Eden to
till it and keep it. *(Gen. 2:8–9, 15)*

For most of the previous two decades, our family lived in northern
New England, either a stone's throw from the Canadian border or
within the sound of the granite shoreline of the Gulf of Maine. We
began gardening there—a small strawberry patch to start, then
peas, squash, and a tomato plant or two. But you can't claim to be a
gardener in those latitudes unless you've planted potato sets in long
rows—and harvested them—which we eventually did. By the time
we were getting the hang of feeding ourselves, we moved south. Or,
rather, to *the* South.

As soon as we got settled in, we began turning over a patch of yard
to start a new garden. Potatoes, at least the species we planted, did
not do well in the blistering heat and the long dry spells of our new
home. The second year we adjusted. Nancy noticed that we really
have two New England summers, back to back, here in Kentucky.

Maybe there was time to get two plantings in parts of the garden during one season? In August, we began clearing the spent cucumber and squash tendrils and got down to the bare earth. The ground was harder than I'd thought dirt could get, having just been turned a few months earlier. More like a ceramic than a clay. I began sinking the blade of my shovel, then lifting and turning the desiccated top soil. It was tough slogging.

Hank, my next-door neighbor, wandered by to see what we were doing. He admired the still productive tomato plants. "The average one needs three gallons of water apiece in this kind of weather," he said in his soft voice. Whenever he makes an observation of this sort, I think what he is really trying to say is, "You beginners better get more water to these tomatoes if you know what's good for them." Hank is a big man, honest and kind, and was both a geologist and a farmer before he got the call to ministry.

He watched me work a moment longer with something of the tender pity the Wampanoags must have felt for the Pilgrims. And, like them, he offered to help. "Would you care to borrow a rototiller?"

I paused with the insole of my shoe resting on the shovel. I thought about all the noise that the machine would make. I considered the pollution that the rototiller would spew, and the gasoline it would use. Taking out a handkerchief to wipe my neck and face, I answered, "Absolutely!"

After the soil was tilled, Nancy and I laid out rows and planted seeds. When I went to water the garden that evening, I sprinkled the freshly cultivated and planted section first, and then I turned my attention toward the carrots and onions. Next, I watered the

---

God's first commandment to mankind was to tend and keep the earth.

"The Lord God took the man and put him in the garden of Eden to till it and keep it" (Gen. 2:15).

section with the peppers. Lastly, I turned the hose on the tomatoes. Part of a full life is watering a verdant tomato plant on a summer's evening—the smell will beguile you. As vesper scents go, it ranks up there somewhere in between just-cut hay and hugging a two-year-old after a bath.

The sun dipped in a cloudless sky, and the day's heat and humidity eased.

That was when it happened. I turned toward the next section of garden and caught a vision of Nancy's footprint in the soil. It wouldn't have been visible if it had not been filled with water from the hose. But there it was: a foot-size lake reflecting the setting sun. I saw it not through my own eyes—but through the eyes of the first gardener. Oh, how much it must have meant for God to wander into the Garden in the evening. A moment through God's eyes is all that we can probably stand, and maybe it is all that is required to set our sights on where we need to go.

God, after all, has the greenest of green thumbs. He is the ultimate horticulturist: *the LORD God planted a garden in Eden*" (Gen. 2:8). It's not surprising that his first commandment to humankind involves gardening: *"The LORD God took the man, and put him into the garden of Eden to dress it and to keep it"* (Gen. 2:15, KJV). Dress and keep a garden. That was the original plan. We were made in God's image. He took soil from the ground, and he molded and spun it into creatures who in some deep sense resemble the kind of God who loves stars and birds and whales and even the creeping ants that make life possible.

Dress and keep a garden (Gen. 2:15). In the original Hebrew tongue, "dress" and "keep" were rendered *"abat"* and *"shimar."* These Hebrew words are variously translated as "dress and keep," "protect and serve," "tend and care." The translations may be

> **The Bible repeatedly affirms that work is not a result of the Fall, but is rather a dignified and essential part of creation.**

slightly different, but the meaning is clear. We are the earth's chosen gardeners. It is the work of our lives.

Like God, we are made to be gardeners. Although we are *"made in God's"* image, that doesn't mean we are miniature versions of a God who is a zillion miles tall and who sneezes when the pollen comes. Rather, it means that at some deep level of our souls we have an impulse to protect the earth. That is what we have been put here to do. We're to tend and till, clean and protect, dress and keep the garden. It is our job. There is no expiration date; God never rescinds this first commandment. How could he? The earth is woven into the fabric of our being. We are inextricably part of this place. We were taken from the soil, and our DNA—like that of grasshoppers, trees, and wombats—all spins in the same direction.

One of the first things that God plants in the Garden is *"every tree that is pleasant to the sight."* When it comes to trees, beauty is not, as the saying goes, relative. The beauty of trees is not in the eyes of the beholder, for *every tree* is pleasing to God's sight. This glimpse into the nature of God is particularly intriguing. Up until this point, God has declared his creation "good." Now he explicitly assigns an aesthetic value: trees are pleasing to his sight. A tree's first order of business is to be beautiful, and next, to produce things that are "good to eat." Aesthetics are cited before the practicality of filling an empty stomach.

Trees play a critical role in the Bible: There is a line of trees that stretches from the Garden of Eden to the center of heaven. In our lives today, trees play just as critical a role. This past summer Nancy

---

Because we disobeyed God, we must work the ground and toil with diminishing productivity. Our disharmony with the Creator and his creation has made our work more difficult and less productive.

"Cursed is the ground because of you; in toil you shall eat of it all the days of your life" (Gen. 3:17).

and I went walking through the city fifteen miles north of our home. It was hot, the middle of the day, with the sun high overhead. Our stroll took us though a well-to-do neighborhood. The houses are large and mostly a century old. It is a nice place to be. What makes the area so pleasant are not the houses but rather the canopy of towering oaks, poplars, and ash trees. They provide a parasol of oxygen-producing chlorophyll that not only cools us but gives the birds a place to nest and the squirrels a commuter byway.

An hour later we were in another part of town. Some refer to it as the wrong side of town. It is not a pleasant place. The sweat ran down our backs. The temperature on the pavement was easily ten degrees higher than in the first neighborhood, just two miles away. What makes this place "poor" and the other neighborhood "rich"? Is it that the homes are small? I don't think so. I am a fan of small homes. It was not the modest homes that made us want to return to the first neighborhood. What was it then?

Poverty. This place is poor, but by a standard other than that of mere money. It is deprived because it has no trees. No trees means no squirrels, no birds, no oxygen-rich air, no shade. No dappled light. No beauty. It is poor when judged by the aesthetic standard in Genesis 2:8–15.

I couldn't help wondering, *What about all the huge churches in the city? Why haven't any of them come to plant trees in this neighborhood?* Beautiful trees were the first gift to us from God. Planting trees would be worthy work for people made in the image of God. It would be one of the few gifts sure to increase in value, get bigger, and give more as the years went by. It is the first job given to humanity—to protect and serve the earth. Is it not the job of the church as well?

> **The relationship between humans and the land is antagonistic because of our sin.**
>
> *"When you till the ground, it will no longer yield to you its strength"* (Gen. 4:12).

The first kind of work an individual or a church should begin with is that of tending the garden. It's biblical—the Genesis 2:15 commandment. I cannot promise that gardening will lead to a moment of rapture such as the one I had standing next to the tomatoes this summer. Those moments are rare, and we cannot conjure up God's presence. As anyone who has ever been transported to Narnia knows, Narnia calls you, not the other way around.

Having said that, of the half dozen such moments I've experienced through God's eyes, two happened while working in a garden. From my informal survey of friends about "God moments," it seems as if they most often occur while one is working, especially when surrounded by the natural world. A survey of the entire Bible reveals that God shows up outdoors more often than indoors. Jesus mostly taught on field trips. By its very nature, gardening takes us outside. One of the most encouraging movements in the church today is community gardening.

It was really Nancy who started us down the gardening path. I resisted. My parents had a garden when I was young. It was large enough to require a tractor's attention in the spring, bounded by a fence with corner posts of wood. The posts were whitewashed and had old license plates nailed over their tops to keep the water out. The fence and the talisman on its corner posts represented the boundaries of our domestic life. Beyond was a field rotated through crops of corn and clover and hay. Past the first field was another, and then a pasture. At the bottom of the grazing hill was a stream that had the power to make children like me fall in it at any time of the year.

I recall one day in particular when I was picking bugs off potato plants. As memory serves me, I was being punished. I wanted to

---

Because of our sin, all of creation suffers.

"We know that the whole creation has been groaning in labor pains"
(Rom. 8:22; see also Gen. 6:7; Lev. 26; Deut. 11:13–17).

escape from my garden chores, and freedom loomed just over the fence. Then it hit me. I couldn't run away. Jim, the character in Twain's novel, was in better condition than I. Slaves had it better. At least they could escape. Jim could hightail it to the Mississippi, but I couldn't. From that moment onward I made it a point to be passively aggressive toward all things pertaining to the garden. And that is the childish mind-set I brought to horticulture when Nancy started our first garden.

My bad attitude was biblical and deserves discussing. I do not know how much of the first few chapters of Genesis are meant to be taken literally and how much is allegorical, but I do know this: to interpret it as anything other than truth is to miss the point. At some time man and woman worked in a garden, and it probably didn't feel like work at all because they knew it was dignified and necessary. I would not be surprised if the "apple" Eve was offered came in the form of a labor-saving device. I'm sure it was over packaged, purchased on credit, and had no payments due until the Fall.

By disobeying God and trying to avoid honest labor, what we got was busy work: *"By the sweat of your face you shall eat bread until you return to the ground"* (Gen. 3:19). *From now on,* a disappointed God cries out, *you guys are going to have to work.* Before the Fall, Adam knew the name of every animal. After the Fall he needed a field guide. If you think this is a bunch of hooey, consider that butterflies with brains the size of a piece of dust can migrate for thousands of miles without using MapQuest. They just know how. There's no study or schooling involved. Yet man, with a brain the size of a duckpin bowling ball, can spend thirteen years in primary and secondary education, four years getting a bachelor's degree, several

---

God wants us to use the land, not abuse it.

"Is it not enough for you to feed on the good pasture, but you must tread down with your feet the rest of your pasture? When you drink of clear water, must you foul the rest with your feet?" (Ezek. 34:18).

more working on a master's, and another three getting a PhD, all in preparation to write a book on butterfly migration. If that's not an example of having to scratch a living from the soil, I don't know what qualifies.

The desire to get out of work is something that seems to be inborn. It is one of the deep, inexplicable results of the Fall. A child will play endlessly with a set of blocks, but cleaning up is a different matter. An adolescent will eat from the garden but not want to pick the bugs off the plants. There is an entire genre of children's books devoted to genies in bottles. They appeal to the fallen three-year-old psyche—not having to clean up, do chores, or go to school. Presto—Shazaam! The work is done. No more toys to pick up, weeds to dig, or dishes to wash. The lure of magic is strong. Magical thinking begins in childhood, but it doesn't end there.

Enter the labor-saving device. They are designed to help us avoid work. And as any son of Adam or daughter of Eve knows, when we don't have to work, we have more time to play. The definition of play is doing what we want—when we want. Yet, oddly, despite all the gadgets, machines, and progress, the battle cry of the modern life is "I'm too busy/I don't have enough time/There aren't enough hours in a day." We don't get together with friends, smell the roses, or learn to paint because we don't have enough time. So what do we do to make things better? Buy more technology to save us more time.

We buy machines that brush our teeth, wash our dirty dishes, and water house plants automatically. We can purchase a tie rack that spins, using a battery, and dispensers that heat hand lotion so we don't have to warm it in our palms. We see ads for a robotic vacuum and a contraption that massages our tired feet. Half-horsepower machines stand ready in kitchens to "instantly" chop carrots.

God wants us to work constructively, not destructively.

"Do not work for the food that perishes, but for the food that endures for eternal life" (John 6:27).

We can have a three-minute egg in just thirty seconds. No need to get up off the couch and change the channel—the remote is in hand. Now, none of these things is inherently evil. God gave us dominion over the things of the earth. The problem begins when *things* get dominion over us. If so many time- and labor-saving devices exist, why does this generation complain of being "out of time"?

I'm not proposing a return to the good old days—just the parts that were better. The good old days were filled with plenty of rotten situations that we can be thankful are gone. I like a world with antibiotics, vaccinations, and opportunity for all. Slavery is one of the labor-saving institutions that I don't wish to come back.

Take the example of St. Patrick. Everyone knows about St. Patrick's inventing green beer and a great holiday where anyone can be Irish. But for half a decade, Patrick was a slave. He was taken from his native home in Britain by a raiding party and held against his will in the emerald countryside of Ireland. He herded sheep (always a good job as far as the Lord is concerned), learned the language, and eventually escaped back to England. What makes Patrick a saint is not the parade or the Chicago River changing color; it's the fact that having been a "labor-saving device" himself, he chose to risk his freedom and very life by going back to his captors. Though I certainly don't condone slavery, I admire Patrick because he was not afraid of work.

Most of us are born with a lazy streak, and the example of St. Patrick teaches us that it is good to work against this tendency.

If our work is done in harmony with his creation, God promises that it will yield great benefits. One reward of hard work is wisdom and respect. The Proverbs 31 wife

"looks well to the ways of her household, and does not eat the bread of idleness" and *"she opens her mouth with wisdom, and the teaching of kindness is on her tongue"* (Prov. 31:27, 26; see also 12:11; 13:4; 14:4; 31:10–27).

My slothful trait is as big as anyone's. For years I've been dreaming about starting a magazine called *Hammock Times*, but I haven't gotten around to it . . . yet.

Rest, when it does come, is ever so much sweeter when our work is accomplished. Sharing work with others eases the burden. Working together is part of God's original plan. According to St. Patrick, it was not so much the slavery that was difficult to endure, but working in isolation from others.

Work is infinitely more meaningful when it is shared. For that matter, probably everything is. We were not built to be alone. God's plan includes companionship, as we work together:

> GOD said, "It's not good for the Man to be alone; I'll make him a helper, a companion." So GOD formed from the dirt of the ground all the animals of the field and all the birds of the air. He brought them to the Man to see what he would name them. Whatever the Man called each living creature, that was its name. The Man named the cattle, named the birds of the air, named the wild animals; but he didn't find a suitable companion.
>
> GOD put the Man into a deep sleep. As he slept he removed one of his ribs and replaced it with flesh. GOD then used the rib that he had taken from the Man to make Woman and presented her to the Man. *(Gen. 2:18–22, MSG)*

Another reward of good work: it strengthens our faith. When we hang laundry on the line or carry dishwater out to moisten the garden, our love for God is made tangible through daily acts of humble service.

"Just as the body without the spirit is dead, so faith without works is also dead" (James 2:26).

The birds at the feeder, the deer in the backyard, and the whales in the sea are all part of God's plan to help us. But we need more. We need one another. Labor can be dreary if done alone. This was true in the Garden even before the Fall or sin came into the world. In taking the rib from Adam's side, the symbol of equal helpmate is emphasized. The helpmate came not from his head (a fantasy) and not from his foot (a servant), but from the very bone of his bone, and flesh of his flesh. The ideal way to labor is side-by-side with one another.

Labor-saving devices contribute to our modern, isolated way of life. When people used to cut wood with a two-person saw, there was teamwork. Now when we cut wood with a chainsaw, there is only deafening noise and choking pollution to keep us company. When people mended clothes in the evenings, there was quiet conversation. Today, sewing is done on a machine, frequently in the basement, alone. When people in the industrialized West stopped getting together to plant a garden, wash clothes, make a quilt, raise a barn, and preserve the autumn harvest, they lost the camaraderie that comes with shared labor.

Labor-saving devices also make us confuse necessities with luxuries. We turn the faucet knob to get water instead of pumping a handle. We throw a switch for heat instead of carrying the wood in and lighting a fire. Water on tap or heat at the flip of a switch are wonderful luxuries, but that's just what they are: luxuries and not necessities. Billions of people before us managed to get through life with fewer luxuries than our generation. They were able to pen books that still enthrall, write songs that continue to uplift, and live lives that keep on inspiring.

> **One of the *greatest* rewards of work is that it allows us to share with others.**
>
> *"Let them labor and work honestly with their own hands, so as to have something to share with the needy"* (Eph. 4:28; see also Prov. 9:1–6).

Labor-saving devices may be useful in moderation, but when used in excess they are counterproductive, both physically and spiritually. The conscious decision to forgo certain devices and objects is the beginning of getting dominion over the things of the earth, rather than allowing things to have dominion over us.

Until eight years ago, our family owned an electric clothes dryer and used it without a second thought. We no longer own a clothes dryer—but we do have one of the most famous clotheslines in the country. It's been filmed and photographed. It's in glossy magazines, newspapers, and documentaries. Until about a hundred years ago, no one on the planet ever had, or needed, an electric clothes dryer. Everybody—rich, poor, old, and young—dried wet clothing the same way: they hung it up on a line. We dry our laundry the way Jesus, Bach, and Einstein did. Only lately has it become news.

The result is that drying clothes on the line makes my family's life a little richer. We started using this retro technology out of a desire to save energy and pollute the earth less. Each load that we dry on the line saves five pounds of coal from being burned back at the electricity plant. Much of America's coal comes from the Appalachian mountains of West Virginia, Virginia, and Kentucky. This area of the country—named after the Apache Indians—is rugged and lush with hardwood forests and wildlife.

Coal is no longer mined through shafts bored into a mountain. The new technique, called mountaintop removal mining, is worse than strip-mining; it entails exploding entire mountains to extract a thin seam of coal. The mountains of Appalachia are formed like a huge layer cake—very skinny layers of coal frosting between rock layers hundreds of feet thick. We're smashing and crushing the entire cake to get at a few thin strips of frosting.

> **Indeed, God wants us to find pleasure in work because dignified labor is part of his plan for creation.**

A modern miner is not a miner at all; rather, he is an "exploder." In West Virginia, three million pounds of ordinance is detonated every day. It is an unrelenting 24/7 assault to remove forest, deer, birds, and several hundred feet of unwanted rock. The goal of mountaintop removal is to arrive at a three-foot seam of coal as quickly as possible.

What is done with all the atomized rock and forest? It, along with billions of tons of debris, is dumped into the valleys. These valleys tend to be graced by babbling brooks filled with fish and other wildlife and make convenient places for coal companies to dump the exploded mountains. Now, if you or I were to shovel tree stumps, slag, and dirt into the Potomac River, we would end up in jail for polluting the water. Here's how the coal companies get around the Clean Water Act: they make the streams vanish! And since a buried stream no longer exists, the coal companies aren't polluting the water.

To date, the legal system has bought this kind of logic to the tune of twelve hundred miles of vanished streams and rivers in the state of West Virginia alone. It would be like holding up a bank and then blowing it up on the way out. "How can my client be guilty of bank robbery?" your attorney would rage. "There isn't even a bank there!"

"There is nothing better for mortals than to eat and drink, and find enjoyment in their toil. This also, I saw, is from the hand of God" (Eccles. 2:24; see also Eccles. 5:12).

"To dress it and keep it."
That, then, was to be our work.

Alas! What work have we set ourselves instead?
How have we ravaged the garden instead of kept it—
Modern Painters V, *John Ruskin (1819–1900)*

"Mountaintop Removal," oddly enough, is a coal company's euphemism. A more accurate term would be "Mountaintop Destruction." In Revelation 11:18, God promises to someday *destroy the destroyers of the earth.* For those of us who take this Scripture seriously, we have ample incentive to do a little work or perhaps make a few sacrifices to cut back on our electricity usage and thereby avoid being responsible for destroying God's mountains.

A typical family uses 1,800 pounds of coal per year powering just its electric clothes dryer. An average of 20,000 pounds of forest, dirt, and rock must be dumped in a stream in order to get that amount of coal. It is easy to rail against greedy corporations and corrupt judges. It's a little harder to actually do something about mountaintop removal by changing our behavior. Hanging the laundry and reducing the need for coal is the work of serving and protecting the earth.

The first reason that my family abandoned the clothes dryer and started using a clothesline was to honor the commandment to tend and care for the garden; however, it is not the primary reason that we continue to do it.

We do this labor-increasing activity because it gives us more life. When I'm outside hanging clothes, I've learned to enjoy the motion of removing articles from the basket and tuning in to the breeze and animals around me in our backyard. I've learned the joy of working with the awareness of God alongside.

When I hang clothes with Nancy or one of the children, I also enjoy companionship. Working side by side, we accomplish one of the beautifully mundane tasks of the day. In the words of the Shaker song, "It is a gift to be simple. It's a gift to be free."

What we work and produce we do not only for ourselves but for our God and our neighbor.

The Way to Christ *3:7, Jacob Boehme (1575–1624)*

These moments together, of just being, are important—just as important to me as saving fish in a mountain stream.

Clothes dryers are the second biggest energy consumer of any home appliance (refrigerators are first). I am all for green power production. But to get drying clothes by hand into perspective, the use of clotheslines nationally would save more energy than all the alternative energy sources (solar, wind, geothermal) in usage today. It seems like such a simple behavior change. The problem? No one has ever made a slick ad for a clothespin. The solution is too simple. A clothesline and clothespins cost less than one hundred dollars. There is no profit in it.

John Wesley, founder of the Methodists, was born at the turn of the seventeenth century. He had, and continues to have, a profound effect on the church and culture. Does your church sing songs that resemble popular tunes? This linking originated with John and his brother Charles. Do you attend a small faith group or Bible study in someone's home? John's doing. Are those without formal theological training allowed to speak in your church? John again. Does your church meet in a school, hotel, or other nonchurch building? John Wesley did it first. He was an innovator even when it came to medicine. In midcareer as an Anglican minister, he took up the practice of medicine and authored a best-selling medical text.

> The idea that the service to God should have only to do with a church altar, singing, reading, sacrifice, and the like is without doubt but the worst trick of the devil. . . . The whole world could abound with the services to the Lord, Gottesdienste—not only in churches but also in the home, kitchen, workshop, field.
>
> What you do in your house is worth as much as if you did it up in heaven for our Lord God.
>
> Works [Erlanger edition], vol. 5, Martin Luther (1483–1546)

At the beginning of his textbook, *Primitive Physic: or, An Easy and Natural Method of Curing Most Diseases*, first published in 1747, Wesley includes a curious comment concerning health, work, and the Bible. He states that we are meant to earn our way by the sweat of our brow. To try and cheat the system not only goes against the wishes of God, it is bad for our health. Some of Wesley's medical cures are out of date or odd, but his recommendation of daily work for spiritual and physical reasons was ahead of its time. That Wesley lived to age eighty-seven in a time of tuberculosis, cholera, and even plague is noteworthy indeed.

I don't believe that Wesley would have been too keen on Western culture's latest aids to sloth. These products—found in nearly every American home—make switching on labor-saving devices look like hard work. I'm speaking of the disposable products—pens, paper towels, plastic cups—that fill our homes, workplaces, and churches, as well as our landfills.

One of the churches that I've had the pleasure to work with is located in Pleasant View, Tennessee. Their members got together one Sunday to discuss how to feed more of the poor in their area. They met over a meal, and as is customary, someone said grace beforehand. Included in the prayer was a comment thanking God for the abundance in their lives and a remembrance of those around the world who didn't have anything to eat at the moment. Then a thought came to someone at the table. They were going to eat their fill and then throw all the utensils, plates, cups, napkins, and table clothes in the garbage. Somewhere along the way they

---

And the earth is not cursed in itself, but is "cursed in your work" (Gen. 3:17, John 6:50). This is said in reference to the soul. The earth is cursed if your works are earthly, that is, of this world. It is not cursed as a whole. It will merely bring forth thorns and thistles if it is not diligently cared for by the labor of human hands.

Paradise, *St. Ambrose of Milan (c. 340–397)*

had gotten too rich, busy, and lazy to put the dirty dishes into the dishwasher.

"How much does all this tableware cost?" someone asked. It turned out that they could feed a family for a year on what they were spending on disposable kitchen items. It also dawned on the men and women present that many of the labor-saving devices invented over the last half century were sold under the guise of "liberation." The men present decided to volunteer as dishwashers for the first year. The proposal was unanimously accepted by the women, and they all began the journey of becoming better tenders of the garden.

This simple act of doing the dishes has led to other acts of service. There seems to be more time and money for helping others. They are learning to garden, compost, and conserve water as a team.

In the Garden of Eden, God gave us a job. That job has dignity attached to it. When we try to cheat God, we end up cheating ourselves—and the generations ahead that will need clean air, water, and land in order to grow and prosper.

Indeed, some of the delicious fruits we've been offered—like labor-saving devices and disposable products—turn out to be filled with worms. It takes an experienced gardener to tell the difference.

Next summer, we are doubling the size of our garden, crossing over to our neighbor Hank's yard. Our families will turn the soil over together. In the spring, we will plant peas. Neighborhood children will join us. That is how God intended—for us to tend and protect the Garden, together.

There is a treasure in the earth of our being that is a food tasty and pleasing to the Lord. Be a gardener. Dig and ditch. Toil and sweat. Turn the earth upside down and seek the "dampness" and water the plants in time. Continue the labor and make sweet floods to run, and noble and abundant fruits to spring forth. Take this food and drink and carry it to God as your true worship.

Showings, *Julian of Norwich (1342–c. 1416)*

Tending the Garden
What you can do to be intentionally green

- Plant shade trees and fruit-bearing bushes and trees.
- Start a vegetable garden.
- Mow the grass with a push mower.
- Collect and take out compost.
- Rake leaves instead of collecting with a blower or mower.
- Hang laundry on the line.
- Wash and dry dishes by hand.
- Collect dishwater and use it to water the garden.
- Walk or ride a bike instead of driving.
- Cook meals at home instead of eating out.
- Pack a lunch for work or school.
- Mend clothes that have holes or small tears.
- Repair leaky faucets.
- Add caulking and weather stripping around windows and doors.
- Slip insulation around hot-water pipes.
- Make curtains for windows.
- Use fewer convenience foods.
- Can and preserve fruits and vegetables in season.
- Make nontoxic cleaning solutions, like vinegar and water.
- Avoid buying anything with the word *disposable*.
- Stock up on cloth hankies.
- Invest in a steel razor and single blades.
- Purchase refillable pencils.
- Make or purchase cloth napkins.

- Clean out plastic bags and aluminum foil and reuse.
- Clean out closets, attics, and basements, and give away what you don't need.
- Shovel the driveway for a neighbor.
- Bake a loaf of bread for someone housebound.
- Recycle religiously.
- Volunteer to be the recycling czar at church or work.
- Collect plastic bottles and cans at sporting events.
- Keep a bag in the car for items that can be recycled later.
- Keep fabric shopping bags in the car, and use them wherever you shop (not just in the grocery store).
- Volunteer to wash dishes at church events.
- Organize a church or community garden, and donate some of the produce to the poor.
- Start a tree-planting campaign for the marginalized sections of town, or start an urban garden.
- Repair, reuse, and make do instead of buying new.

Adapted with permission from Go Green, Save Green: A Simple Guide to Saving Time, Money and God's Green Earth *(Nancy Sleeth, Tyndale, 2009). For more ideas, visit www.blessedearth.org.*

Water
The Flood

The Lᴏʀᴅ saw that the wickedness of humankind was great in the earth, and that every inclination of the thoughts of their hearts was only evil continually. And the Lᴏʀᴅ was sorry that he had made humankind on the earth, and it grieved him to his heart. . . . Then the Lᴏʀᴅ said to Noah, "Go into the ark, you and all your household, for I have seen that you alone are righteous before me in this generation. Take with you seven pairs of all clean animals, the male and its mate; and a pair of the animals that are not clean, the male and its mate; and seven pairs of the birds of the air also, male and female, to keep their kind alive on the face of all the earth. For in seven days I will send rain on the earth for forty days and forty nights; and every living thing that I have made I will blot out from the face of the ground."

And Noah did all that the Lᴏʀᴅ had commanded him.

(Gen. 6:5–6; 7:1–5)

I was in the middle of a long shift in the emergency room. Nothing much was happening. Most of the time that I spent moonlighting at this quiet hospital—a change of pace from the busy ER where I usually worked—involved "dozing for dollars." The job was difficult only because of the tedious hours of isolation. A twenty-four- or forty-eight-hour shift seemed a lifetime of separation from family, home, and friends. I would leave these shifts humming the line from a country song, "I turned twenty-one in prison doing life without parole."

It was on one of these long shifts that I saw my first floppy baby. In medical parlance, that's what we call an infant without muscle tone, a baby that does not cry. A floppy baby slumbers somewhere between earth and heaven, life and death, and triumph and tragedy. It strikes terror in the hearts of doctors and nurses, not to mention mothers and fathers. Even those who do not believe in God pray when they see a child in this condition.

I was called over to an examination table by a fireman—not a paramedic—who had brought in the dying baby. The firefighter looked uncomfortably overdressed in his thick coat and crash helmet—the infant so pale and fragile in his large hands.

I listened with my stethoscope to the still, four-month-old chest. I heard nothing. The nurse slashed away with orange-handled trauma scissors at the infant's cotton onesy outfit. I listened over the child's mouth. Nothing. I laid my ear in the middle of the child's small chest. Something—a thready, rapid, ever-so-faint heartbeat.

Placing my lips over the nose and mouth of the child, I exhaled. In my peripheral vision, I saw the little chest rise. Doctors in America nearly always operate and examine from the right side of the patient. Somehow I had found myself working from the infant's left side. Like the fact that it was a firefighter rather than a paramedic who brought in the baby, this is one of those odd, jarring details that stayed with me: I was working on the wrong side of baby John Doe.

According to the first creation story in Genesis, the earth itself was formed by God out of the waters.

"In the beginning when God created the heavens and the earth, the earth was a formless void and darkness covered the face of the deep, while a wind from God swept over the face of the waters" (Gen. 1:1–2).

This infant appeared to be dying from dehydration—the most common cause of childhood death around the world. What was needed, what could save this little one's life, was a pint of IV fluids. It is difficult to start an IV in a severely dehydrated adult, and it is nearly impossible to do so in a dying infant. Yet doctors have a way around the standard IV insertion, which takes into account the unique anatomy of a child. With the help of an interosseous trocar—a tool that has a handle and a hollow, pointed tube about the size and length of a 12-penny nail—the doctor can use force to drive a hole through the skin and into the baby's tibia. Once the physician punctures the bone, vast amounts of fluid can then be pushed directly into the marrow and subsequently absorbed into the body.

Just a week prior, a doctor noticed that there was no interosseous trocar in the ER. She said something about it to the head nurse, who—though the tool is rarely used—promptly ordered one. Lying on a desk just around the corner was a brand-new trocar wrapped in a sterile container. Someone ran to get it.

By this time, news of the floppy baby had traveled through the hospital. Nurses from various departments had come to help, along with the on-call family doctor. Someone from the lab held empty vials. The radiology technician stood by a portable x-ray machine, wearing a blue leaded apron.

The baby, apparently abandoned, had arrived with no history, no parents in tow. Quick action was needed or we would lose what little hope remained. I remember the amount of pressure that it took for me to push the trocar through the little shin bone, and how relieved I felt when the water of life flowed from a saline bag into the child.

> **God first separates the waters above from the waters below; then God creates the earth out of the waters.** Once the earth is formed, he places all living things, including humans, on earth—all dependent on water for continued life.

In seeing thirty thousand patients in the ER, I was only called twice to perform this emergency procedure. Once, by God's grace, we saved the baby's life. This time, we did not. The baby perished for want of a glassful of fluid.

Water is essential. We need water to survive, yet the historical relationship between humanity and water has been far from benign. Of all the elements in Genesis, water is the one that God does not declare "good." To the ancient people, water represented danger, chaos, and darkness.

Noah lived untold centuries in the past. Many believe that he dwelled with his family in the broad lush flatlands between the Tigris and Euphrates rivers.

When my son was born, friends gave him a baby quilt embroidered with a picture of the ark. Noah stands by his ark, with pairs of giraffes and hippopotamuses trotting down a gangplank. Overhead, a huge rainbow reflects rays of light in water droplets. This quilted portrayal is how we often think of Noah—as a kind of bearded, friendly zookeeper.

The flood story we heard in childhood focuses on cuddly animals and the prismatic rainbow. But there is another, darker side to the story. Noah lived in the most difficult of times. Every human heart was turned toward greed and selfishness. Reread Homer—throwing babies off the wall was commonplace in ancient times. Infant and child sacrifice was the norm.

A communal effort to save an unknown infant such as the one

Just as the earth is born out of the waters, so is each individual. Not only do babies develop for nine months in the womb's water, but each of us is called to be reborn as a Christian in the living waters. As Jesus said to Nicodemus,

"No one can enter the kingdom of God without being born of water and Spirit" (John 3:5).

described in the beginning of this chapter would have made no sense to the people of Noah's day. Might made right. Go out for a gallon of milk, and you might never come home. An encounter with anyone bigger or better armed could result in death or permanent enslavement. We can hardly imagine the total lack of respect of another's personhood and the harsh conditions that prevailed.

"The LORD was sorry that he had made humankind on the earth, and it grieved him in his heart" (Gen. 6:6). The state of civilization had sunk so low that God decided to close up the show. Fortunately, there was one upright family. Noah and his family found favor in God's eyes.

The flood is a story of God reacting to evil—a story of redemption. In the past, God made a covenant with mankind through Adam. Now he is making a new covenant with Noah.

Imagine that you are going to another planet. What would you take? Would you bring your television, your automobile, or your toaster oven? If I were sent off to an unknown future on an uncharted planet, I would like to bring the earth's greatest treasure. I would bring what God bequeathed to Noah, and to us. I would bring the animals.

> **The miracles of creation and life are just two of the many miracles associated with water.** The flood and the subsequent redemption (Gen. 6-9), the preservation of the infant Moses (Exod. 2), the plagues in Egypt (Exod. 7–10), the dividing of the Red Sea (Exod. 14), the water from the rock (Exod. 17), the dividing of the Jordan River (Josh. 3), Elijah and the drought (1 Kings 17–18), the consumption of Elijah's water-drenched altar (1 Kings 18), Elisha and the floating ax head (2 Kings 6), Jesus' turning water into wine (John 2), the great catches of fish (Luke 5; John 21), Jesus' walking on water (Matthew 14), and Jesus' calming the stormy seas (Mark 4) all show God using water as evidence of his presence and power.

Once Noah built the ark and sheltered the animals, God opened the floodgates, and the waters poured forth. A flood is the most primordial of events. It is always terrifying. Yet there came a day when the rain ceased, the sun came out, and the wind blew. Noah released a raven. When the bird failed to return, he released a dove.

In ecological terms, birds have always been of tremendous significance. William McDonough, the Green Dean of American architecture, measures the success of his buildings by the number of songbirds that come to dwell in and around his projects.

When the flood recedes, God uses a bird to symbolize hope and restoration. Perhaps one of the most beautiful images in the Bible is the dove returning to Noah with an olive branch in its beak. The olive tree is one of the most useful trees to humanity. It provides oil, fruit, wood, and shade. It is also one of the longest lived trees on the earth. Some specimens have been dated to a thousand years of age or more.

Noah sees that the world is fresh and clean and a rainbow appears in the sky. The next order of business is to get the animals outside.

God said to Noah, "Go out of the ark, you and your wife, and your sons and your sons' wives with you. Bring out with you every living thing that is with you of all flesh—birds and animals and every creeping thing that creeps on the earth—so that they may abound on the earth, and be fruitful and multiply on the earth." So Noah went out with his sons and his wife and his sons' wives. And every animal, every creeping thing, and every bird, everything that moves on the earth, went out

---

Scripture repeatedly reminds us to be grateful for the miracle of water in our daily lives. Water is a gift from God:

"He does great things and unsearchable, marvelous things without number. He gives rain on the earth and sends waters on the fields" *(Job 5:9–10).*

of the ark by families. I have set my bow in the clouds, and
it shall be a sign of the covenant between me and the earth.
When I bring clouds over the earth and the bow is seen in the
clouds, I will remember my covenant that is between me and
you and every living creature of all flesh; and the waters shall
never again become a flood to destroy all flesh. (Gen. 8:15–19;
9:13–15)

God makes a covenant with the animals. He instructs them to be
fruitful and multiply and to fill the earth. In a moment Noah and
his family will worship God, but before worship comes the care of
animals. This ethic will repeat itself again and again throughout the
Scriptures. Compassion for animals is common among the good
guys, but not among the bad ones. One of the surest signs that a
biblical figure is a player in God's redemptive plan is the person's
decency to the beasts of the field. Humane treatment of animals is
seen here with Noah and will be repeated by Moses, Rebecca, Laban,
and a host of others. It is not a coincidence that Christ is referred to
as the "Good Shepherd."

For the Christian, the events in Genesis are the beginning of a
re-creation of the earth. Humans have fallen from grace. We have
lost the close and easy relationship that we once enjoyed with our
Creator. And it is not just humans who have paid the price for this

**The Psalms tell us not to take water for granted, but to cherish
it.** In Psalms 65, 104, and 107, we are reminded that God provides
water not only for humans but for all of his creatures:

*"You make springs gush forth in the valleys; they flow between the
hills, giving drink to every wild animal; the wild asses quench their
thirst. By the streams the birds of the air have their habitation;
they sing among the branches. From your lofty abode you water the
mountains; the earth is satisfied with the fruit of your work"* (Ps.
104:10–13).

breach. The very earth and its plants and animals are affected. "All of creation groans," as Paul puts it in his letter to the Christians in Rome (Rom. 8:19–23). God is willing to do anything to repair this rift. We are not capable of healing it ourselves. Inherent in our fallen state is an enmity with all things made by the Creator. The image of God in our hearts allows us to feel compassion for living things; our fallen state makes our hearts cold, our eyes blind, and our ears deaf.

In the beginning God walked with humans in the Garden. Our first notion of God was, and is, via his creation. The earth sustains us, glorifies God, and allows for an understanding of the Creator. It is a triad relationship.

Perhaps the greatest reason we should cherish water is that water is a symbol of God. God is the *"drink from the river"* and the *"fountain of life"* (Ps. 36:8–9). He is the *"living water"* that never leaves us thirsty (John 4:10–14). God cleanses us through the waters of baptism: "wash yourselves; make yourselves clean."

Indeed, one way we can

"cease to do evil, learn to do good; seek justice, rescue the oppressed, defend the orphan" (Isa. 1:16–17)

is by becoming better stewards of God's life-giving waters.

What a thing it is to sit absolutely alone, in the forest, at night, cherished by this wonderful, unintelligible, perfectly innocent speech, the most comforting speech in the world, the talk that rain makes by itself all over the ridges, and the talk of the watercourses everywhere in the hollows. Nobody started it, nobody is going to stop it. It will talk as long as it wants, this rain. As long as it talks, I am going to listen.

Raids on the Unspeakable, *Abbey of Gethsemani,*
Thomas Merton (1915–1968)

In the opening of his letter to the Romans, Paul states that we are responsible for our understanding of God even if we have never heard or read a bit of Scripture. Go outside and take a walk, look around, observe nature, and you'll know God, Paul asserts. *"Ever since the creation of the world his eternal power and divine nature, invisible though they are, have been understood and seen through the things he has made. So they are without excuse"* (Rom. 1:20).

But what understanding of God's nature do we obtain from the element of water? Water has the power to both take and give life.

"Let the waters bring forth swarms of living creatures" (Gen. 1:20). We humans share the same percentage of salinity as the sea—as evidenced in the saltiness of our tears, the taste of blood, and the water of our mother's womb. Water that is in the right place, in the right amount, and of the right purity makes life possible, but if water is present in excess, shortage, or impurity, life becomes impossible.

For Christians, the story of the Old Testament is the working of God to bring about the re-creation of the world through the life, death, and rebirth of Jesus. The New Testament shares the details of the work of the Messiah: Jesus Christ of Nazareth.

I've heard a modern joke about the emphasis on teaching about Jesus in Sunday schools. The story begins with the instructor asking a question,

> *We are deeply worried to see that entire peoples, millions of human beings, have been reduced to destitution and are suffering from hunger and disease because they lack drinking water. In fact, hunger and many diseases are closely linked to drought and water pollution. In places where rain is rare or the sources of water dry up, life becomes more fragile; it fades away to the point of disappearing.*
>
> *Speech in Brazil, Lenten Message, 1993,*
> *Pope John Paul II (1920–2005)*

"Class, can anyone tell me what has a brown bushy tail, lives in a tree, and collects nuts?" There is a long silence. The students glance from one to another. They examine the teacher's face, looking for a hint. The silence grows awkward.

Ashley eventually raises her hand, "Teacher, I know the right answer is 'Jesus,' but it sure sounds like a squirrel."

In some real sense, Ashley is right in wanting to answer "Jesus." The gospel of John begins in pure poetry. It also explains the logic behind Ashley's answer.

"In the beginning was the Word, and the Word was with God, and the Word was God. He was in the beginning with God. All things came into being through him, and without him not one thing came into being. What has come into being in him was life, and the life was the light of all people. The light shines in the darkness, and the darkness did not overcome it" (John 1:1–5).

John's gospel does not begin by recounting Jesus' earthly ancestry; it goes back to "the beginning" and asserts that Jesus, "the Word," is the very reason that life and matter exist. He is the nuclear weak force, the nuclear strong force, gravity, electromagnetism, and DNA all rolled into one. He is the cosmic glue, the stuff that holds the universe together. How we feel about water, our neighbor, and a sparrow ultimately gets at how we feel about Christ.

The Word goes even further than how we feel—it is also about how we act. The emphasis on the many roles of Christ, as well as his central part in the miracle of life, is illustrated by a number of his names.

> *I crossed a place where a stream flows underground,*
> *And the sounds of the hidden water*
> *And the water come to light braided in my ear.*
> *I think the maker is here, creating his hill*
> *As it will be, out of what it was.*
>
> Meditation in the Spring Rain, *Wendell Berry (1934–)*

He is:

The root of Jesse
The vine
The Alpha and Omega
The Lamb that takes away the sins of the world
The firstborn of all creation
The Author of life
The morning star
The seed of Abraham
The Good, Great, and Chief Shepherd
The living water.

Less than 1 percent of the water on the earth is contained in lakes, rivers, and wetlands. About 96.3 percent is found in oceans, and the great bulk of the remaining fresh water is locked up in glaciers, ice caps, the atmosphere, and ground moisture. The amount of fresh water available to humans is less than 1 percent of the planet's total water supply. Water, water everywhere, and not much to drink. The gospel of John uses over twenty references to water. Living water—the kind that you or I can drink—is relatively rare.

"I did not take a shower alone this morning." When I announce this in a church, I get people's attention. Whom did Dr. Sleeth take a shower with? The answer, as Ashley from the Sunday school illustration knows, is Jesus. That is why I take a short shower and use a low-flow showerhead. But I still take a shower. When my kids brush their teeth, they turn off the water, but I still want them to brush. Our toilets still flush, but one is a dual-flush model, and the other has a gallon jug and two bricks in the tank displacing half the tank's

> All things flow constantly from God, as water flows from a spring, and tends ever to return to Him as water tends ever to return to its level.
> The Division of Nature, *John Scotus Eriugena (c. 810–877)*

volume. We have a rain barrel that stores a thousand gallons that is used to water the garden.

We don't buy bottled water, but we do filter what comes out of the tap. If the grass turns brown, so be it. If you live in an area where grass will not recover after a prolonged dry spell, then God designed something else to grow there. We are never alone. The God who is always with me cares about how much water I consume, and how much I leave for my neighbors.

Some parts of the world are blessed with an abundance of fresh water, but many are not. From poor areas of Central Asia, where lakes and rivers have dried up, to the wealthy southwestern United States, where the once mighty Colorado River no longer flows to the sea, clean water has increasingly become a significant health concern. In Beijing, the groundwater level has been dropping about six feet every year. Because of increasing population and industrial demands, more than a third of the city's wells have dried up.

Why conserve water? One might as well ask why not light the altar candles using twenty-dollar bills? Without water, life itself is not possible.

Last spring I was teaching in a seminary in New Jersey, speaking to students from around the globe. The discussion turned to the differences between the culture here and abroad.

A soft-spoken graduate student from Korea related that she came from a rural farming district. "It is a simple lifestyle my family lives." She paused and collected her thoughts. "We farm without our own tractor. Our house is small, and we don't have electricity. What I find the oddest about living in the United States," and here

---

Praised be my Lord for our sister water, who is very serviceable unto us,
and humble and precious and clean.
                    Canticle of the Sun, *St. Francis of Assisi (1182–1226)*

she hesitated. Her face grew red with embarrassment, and then she pushed ahead, "What is the strangest thing to me . . . is emptying my bladder in drinking water."

It took a moment to register. We have so much of the stuff (drinking water) that we are literally throwing it down the drain. Brush your teeth and flush the toilet once—and you have just consumed the daily allotment of water for the average Third Worlder.

When Jesus started his three-year ministry, he went down to the Jordan River where he met John the Baptist. This was not the first time he and John met each other. Shortly after Jesus' mother, Mary, conceived, she went to visit Elizabeth. Elizabeth was pregnant with John the Baptist. We are told that baby John leaped in utero when he heard the voice of Mary—the first recorded incident of John and Jesus coming into contact, both still swimming in the salty waters of the womb. We have no other recorded meeting between them in the Bible until Jesus comes to the Jordan River as a thirty-year-old adult to be baptized by John.

John is the first prophet to appear in Israel in four centuries. He is no mincer of words, nor does he pull his punches. John the Baptist taught on the shore of the seventy-mile-long Jordan River. This river marks the eastern border of Israel and, like the Red Sea, it was once parted by God—to allow Joshua and the Israelites to cross into the Promised Land. I would not be surprised if John the Baptist went about his teaching and baptizing near the same stretch of river that God once parted for Joshua's troops.

Here is an example of John's preaching:

Truths are first clouds; then rain, then harvest and food.
Life Thoughts Gathered from the Extemporaneous Discourses of Henry Ward Beecher, *Henry Ward Beecher (1813–1887)*

"You brood of snakes! Who warned you to flee God's coming judgment?

Prove by the way you live that you have really turned from your sins and turned to God. Don't just say, 'We're safe—we're the descendants of Abraham.' That proves nothing. God can change these stones here into children of Abraham. Even now the ax of God's judgment is poised, ready to sever your roots. Yes, every tree that does not produce good fruit will be chopped down and thrown into the fire."

The crowd asked, "What should we do?"

John replied, "If you have two coats, give one to the poor. If you have food, share it with those who are hungry."

Even corrupt tax collectors came to be baptized and asked, "Teacher, what should we do?" *(Luke 3:7–12, NLT)*

John's fiery and convicting sermon is as far from today's comfortable prosperity gospel as a message can get. No one can claim redemption merely by the pew in which one sits. When asked, "What should we do?" John answers, "Make sure *your neighbor* has their best life now!"

Jesus of Nazareth is baptized in the Jordan by John. This is the last recorded time that John will see Jesus alive. As payment for ush-

---

At Blackwater Pond the tossed waters have settled
after a night of rain.
I dip my cupped hands. I drink
a long time. It tastes
like stone, leaves, fire. It falls cold
into my body, waking the bones. I hear them
deep inside me whispering
oh what is that beautiful thing that just happened?

At Blackwater Pond, *Mary Oliver (1935–)*

ering in the King of Peace, John will be imprisoned and beheaded. God's work can be fatal for those who carry it out.

It is hard to imagine that Christ was baptized in polluted water, but no one knows for sure. We do know that at one time none of the water on this planet had been polluted by mankind. The last chapter on the last page of the Bible provides a description of heaven. It does not describe a place in the clouds, but rather an earthly place where all the nations gather on the shores of the river of the waters of life. All are healed by the leaves of the tree of life. The water in heaven is clear and unpolluted; the contaminants are zero parts per million.

During his ministry, Christ is asked many questions. More often than not, he responds with another question: Whose baptism was it? What does the Law of Moses say? How do you read it? Whose picture is on the coin? So many of the questions put to him are not really questions at all, but people being foolish, or contrary. But one day, after Jesus had been praying, one of the disciples approaches and asks a zinger, "Lord, will you teach us how to pray the way that John taught his disciples?"

After being asked so many "Jesus, can I ride in the front seat?" and "Jesus, can I have the first piece of pie?" types of questions, the Messiah immediately offers a straightforward reply. This time, instead of asking the questioner a question, he answers like a kindly teacher giving a review before the final exam. I can hear him prefacing his answer with, "I'll wait until everybody has pencil and paper ready—this will be on the test." Then he teaches humanity how to pray: *"Our Father who art in heaven, hallowed be thy name. Thy kingdom come. Thy will be done, on earth as it is in heaven"* (Matt. 6:9–10; see also Luke 11:2).

Thy kingdom come, thy will be done, on earth as it is in heaven.

On earth as it is in heaven

On Earth

As it is in Heaven

In heaven the water is unpolluted.

Jesus began his teaching the moment he entered the River Jordan. He said, "I am the living water." He got his temple tax from the mouth of a fish. He chose sailors as his followers. Once, on the Sea of Galilee, the waters became so turbulent that his followers became frightened. They woke the sleeping Jesus. Christ put out his hand and spoke to the sea. He calmed the waters with a word. The disciples had witnessed him performing many other miracles. Still, they had not gotten the divinity of the man they followed. Finally, they understood. They understood in the language that they knew best—the language of water. This! This is the Messiah who can master the waters!

Jesus spoke then, as He speaks now, through the language of the earth. *"All things came into being through him, and without him not one thing came into being."*

Would the river of life be the river of life if it had soda bottles floating on it, phosphates dumped into it, and dead fish washing up on its shores?

We often find it difficult to keep our hearts and minds in a grateful posture regarding God's gifts—he has given us so much. The gift of life is the gift of water. Water is an analog of our souls' dependence upon the Lord. Water is not something we can drink a dozen gallons of one day and then go without for weeks. It is a type of daily bread—something we require on an ongoing basis.

"Is it not enough for you to drink clear water? Must you also muddy the rest with your feet? Must my flock feed on what you have trampled and drink what you have muddied with your feet?" (Ezek. 34:18–19, NIV).

Over a billion people—almost one in five people in the world—lack access to clean water. With 60 percent of infant mortality in the world related to lack of clean water, must 1.5 million children under the age of five—like my John Doe floppy baby—continue to die each year for lack of a glass of clear water?

Jesus asks us to live mindful lives. Every time we drink water, every time we wash dishes, every time we brush your teeth—it is an opportunity to think. Think about how we should treat water as a gift, not an entitlement. Think about how conserving water can help us show our love for God the Creator and our global neighbors. As stewards of God's gifts, we are instructed to use water as a daily symbol—as a monastic reminder of our spiritual lives in Christ.

Tending the Garden
What you can do to conserve water

- Turn off the faucet while shaving and brushing teeth.
- Cut shower time by at least three minutes.
- Take showers instead of baths.
- Install low-flow showerheads and sink-faucet aerators.
- Fix leaky faucets and toilets.
- If you have an older toilet that uses three gallons or more per flush, place several liter bottles filled with water in the tank to displace some of the water.
- Only run the dishwasher and clothes washer when full.
- Wash dishes by hand, and collect dishwater in a tub.
- Use dishwater to water plants.
- Store filtered water in the refrigerator rather than waiting for tap water to run cold or purchasing bottled water.
- When shaving, collect water while waiting for it to run warm, and use the collected water on house plants.
- Wear pants and skirts several times before washing.
- Purchase a front-load washing machine.
- Compost instead of using the garbage disposal.
- Plant native, drought-resistant plants.
- Water plants early in the morning or late in the evening to reduce evaporation.
- If you use a hose, put a nozzle on the end so you don't leave water running unnecessarily.
- Check the forecast before you water; don't water if they are calling for rain.

- Naturalize part of your yard, so it doesn't need watering at all.

- Install rain barrels or cisterns to collect water off your roof.

- Use drip irrigation rather than sprinklers to water the garden.

- Use mulch to prevent evaporation in the garden.

- Build up your garden soil with compost and organic matter to hold moisture.

- Plant vegetables close together to provide shade and avoid moisture loss.

- Allow your grass to grow longer. Cutting it short encourages growth, which requires more water.

- When cutting the lawn, leave the clippings on the ground.

- Place an insulated cover over swimming pools when not in use.

- When cleaning outside, use a broom instead of a power washer.

- Think before you buy anything, and buy used when possible. Most items use huge quantities of water in the manufacturing process.

Adapted with permission from Go Green, Save Green: A Simple Guide to Saving Time, Money and God's Green Earth *(Nancy Sleeth, Tyndale, 2009). For more ideas, visit www.blessedearth.org.*

Hospitality

Abraham and the Angels

The LORD appeared unto him in the plains of Mamre: and he sat in the tent door in the heat of the day; and he lifted up his eyes and looked, and, lo, three men stood by him: and when he saw them, he ran to meet them from the tent door, and bowed himself toward the ground, and said, My LORD, if now I have found favour in thy sight, pass not away, I pray thee, from thy servant: Let a little water, I pray you, be fetched, and wash your feet, and rest yourselves under the tree: And I will fetch a morsel of bread, and comfort ye your hearts; after that ye shall pass on: for therefore are ye come to your servant. And they said, So do, as thou hast said. And Abraham hastened into the tent unto Sarah, and said, Make ready quickly three measures of fine meal, knead it, and make cakes upon the hearth. And Abraham ran unto the herd, and fetcht a calf tender and good, and gave it unto a young man; and he hasted to dress it. And he took butter, and milk, and the calf which he had dressed, and set it before them; and he stood by them under the tree, and they did eat. *(Gen. 18:1–8, KJV)*

I have a friend from Africa who is the youngest of four. We were lunching one day, when she related an experience from her graduate-school days in the United States. Picture a gracious PhD professor telling this tale, in a beautiful, dignified Kenyan accent:

"I was taking a seminar in intercultural studies," she began, "with another woman from Africa. We went to our professor's office to pick up our papers. He didn't have them but said they were at his home. The professor then asked if we'd care to drop by his house that evening and pick them up. My friend and I agreed.

"We arrived at the appointed hour and rang the doorbell. After a considerable time, the professor's wife answered. She didn't open the door but spoke through an intercom.

"'Who is it?'

"We explained that we were the professor's students and had come for our papers. There was a long delay, and then she replied, 'Hold on.'

"Eventually the door opened to reveal an annoyed woman. She reluctantly showed us into the house and led us to a large formal living room. 'My husband is busy and will see you shortly,' she said.

"We were asked to sit on an enormous couch in the living room. We could hear our professor and his wife whispering in the next room. Then it was quiet—except for the noise of them eating.

"My friend and I sat there in utter awkwardness. We didn't know what to do. We couldn't talk because they were not talking, and they could hear anything we might say. It seemed like forever, but we had watches on and knew that it was not. About half an hour later, we heard dishes being cleared. Next our teacher walked out of the dining room.

"'I'm sorry to keep you waiting,' he said. 'We were just getting dinner ready when you came.'

The Bible is filled with examples of hospitality. In ancient times, hospitality was considered a highly moral act of neighborliness and mutual aid. From the account of Abraham, Sarah, and the angels (Genesis 17–18) to the story of the widow of Zarephath and Elijah (1 Kings 17), we are exhorted to welcome the stranger into our homes and our lives.

"Then he said something trying to make it better, but he really made the situation worse.

"'We would have invited you to eat with us—but we only had two steaks.'"

Still incredulous all these years later, my friend's eyes grew wide as she shared the story of the inhospitable professor.

Contrast her account with Abraham's reception of the three angels. The moment the stranger, the acquaintance, or the needy show up on Abraham's doorstep, he and Sarah are hosts. Their calf gets turned into steaks. If there are not enough steaks, the steaks are chopped into stew.

The call to be hospitable did not just apply in Abraham's time; shortly after the sacrifice of Jesus, the book of Acts ups the ante, calling us not just to open our homes, but to share all things in common. Today, most of us think of hospitality as inviting the neighbors over for dinner or offering doughnuts and coffee after the church service. But hospitality in both the Old Testament and New Testament encompasses so much more. In fact, it includes not only the whole world, but the world itself.

This connection between hospitality and stewardship will become more clear as I retell Abraham's encounter with the three angels under the oaks of Mamre through a modern, interpretive lens. Ancient texts were not always ancient—at one time they were contemporary accounts of contemporaneous events. Because Jews in the Diaspora did not understand Hebrew, when rabbis read the Torah, they translated on the fly, updating the text with

Throughout much of the Old Testament, the Hebrew people are aliens in strange lands, a reminder of our dependence on God and the earth he created. The God of Moses is one *"who loves the strangers, providing them food and clothing."* His people *"shall also love the stranger, for you were strangers in the land of Egypt"* (Deut. 10:18–19).

contemporary language. Such nonliteral, extended paraphrases are called Targums.

I want to use a Targum here so that we better understand why hospitality is at its most basic level a green issue and why the call to be hospitable applies just as much today for the family living in the gated community—or trailer park—as it did outside of Abraham and Sarah's tent. Until recently, hospitality was embraced as a normative Christian practice. In the last century, however, hospitality has been increasingly marginalized and specialized. Hospitals nurse the sick. The hospitality industry takes in travelers. Hospice cares for the terminally ill. Yet in the fullest sense preached by Paul, Augustine, Luther, Calvin, and Wesley, Christian hospitality is not something that can be delegated to others or accomplished by writing a check to a homeless shelter or refugee organization—although contributions of money and time to such organizations are valued and valuable. Hospitality as a way of life should be at the very core of what it means to be a practicing Christian. Jesus is the host, guest, and meal all in one.

The following Targum teaches us how to practice hospitality today in a have-it-my-way world:

Abe looks up at the still limbs of the oaks that shade his modest ranch home. Out toward the horizon the highway shimmers in the heat. Abraham squints. He thinks he sees three motorcyclists in the distance.

A few minutes later the motorcycles pull up in his driveway. Kickstands are lowered, and the bikes are leaned to the side. The two men on the outside remove their helmets. The one

> **The Bible repeatedly encourages us to open our hearts, homes, and resources to foreigners in our midst.**
>
> *"Do not neglect to show hospitality to strangers, for by doing that some have entertained angels without knowing it" (Heb. 13:2).*

in the middle begins pulling at gloved fingers and removing his leather outer garments. Finally he slips off his bandanna, revealing a shaved head. Abraham catches a glimpse of himself in one of their mirrored sunglasses.

What would you do?
I can tell you what I would say and what residents of the last three suburban developments the bikers visited said. I'd ask, "Can I help you?" in that tone that really says, "What are you doing on my lawn?" But Abe loves God. He does not think of it as *his* lawn; he knows that everything belongs to God.

Abe rushes forward, ignoring the arthritis in his left knee. "Welcome! You fellas look like you've come quite a ways. We're just about to have dinner. Can you join us?"

The biker with "Gabe" embroidered on his vest removes his shades and smiles. The three strangers follow Abe into the kitchen.

"Sarah, we've got guests! Can you whip up some of your special chicken casserole?" She looks up at Abe and then instinctively glances at the outdoor thermometer on the wall. It reads 104°. She hesitates, then gets up and turns on the oven.

"They must be thirsty," Sarah mutters. She reaches into the refrigerator and takes out three longneck bottles.

Abe opens the drinks and passes them around. He puts out some cheese and crackers, then excuses himself to set the table while Sarah makes dinner. The three travelers look up at Abe and Sarah hard at work to please their guests. Life is good. God is in Hebron, and all is right with the universe.

Again, in Paul's letter to the Romans, he urges us to

"extend hospitality to strangers" (Rom. 12:13) while Peter tells us to "offer hospitality to one another without grumbling" (1 Pet. 4:9, NIV).

What can we learn from this Targum of Abraham's story? Angels can show up at the front door. I see no reason, verses, or theology present in the Bible that say this cannot happen to you or me today. They probably won't show up in flowing white robes with flapping wings—nor will we recognize them as the characters from the original Bible verses.

One of two things occurs when God or his ambassadors put in an appearance (a theophany). Humans are scared out of their wits, or they don't recognize whom they are talking to. Jesus assures us that the latter is more likely to occur (Matt. 25:35–46). God most often appears in a form we don't appreciate.

Abraham and Sarah make God the master of the house not by discernment but by force of habit. We are given a similar opportunity every time we welcome someone new into our midst. Chest butting—looking for the differences in our politics, worship, or baseball team affiliations, rather than common ground—rarely uncovers an angel. It is not that Jesus is incapable of showing up as the new neighbor asking to borrow a cup of sugar—it's just that he's more likely to show up from a war-torn country with no clothes, no food, no job, no English, and no place to lay his head.

What does Jesus wear when he arrives at your door? It's a safe bet he's lost the robe he wears in most of his movies. If you're wearing pants, he's got on a skirt. If you've got a beard, he's probably clean shaven. If you look hip, most likely his clothes are a decade out of style.

Maybe you think that it was easier for Sarah and Abraham to welcome the strangers because they lived in a modest neighborhood rather than a gated community. Or because they weren't about to head out for their daughter's soccer game. Or because they weren't

> **Indeed, hospitality is considered an important indicator of a life well lived.** A worthy widow is one who has "shown hospitality" (1 Tim. 5:10).

barely scraping by on food stamps. It's not always easy to have guests. They can be loud. Inconsiderate. Unappreciative. Indeed, living a hospitable life can be costly and inconvenient. It can require sacrifice.

But hospitality isn't about us. It's about others. It's about giving and expecting nothing in return. It's about using less so there will be enough for everyone. It's about being a good steward of resources so there will be plenty for all.

Perhaps it's easiest to see the link between hospitality and good stewardship by looking at what both are not. Both are not about material gain. Both are not about acquisitiveness. Both are not about selfish living, having it all, or expressing a my-way-or-the-highway attitude.

Back in the book of Genesis, God will inquire about Sarah. He will tell Abraham that Sarah will conceive. She will deliver a boy the next summer. Sarah overhears this prophecy from the kitchen window and laughs out loud. It is not the first LOL, but it is the one that echoes down through history. The son will be named "he laughs," pronounced "Isaac" in Hebrew.

Whether through Sarah or her servant Hagar, billions of us around the globe trace our lineage to Abraham. Jews, Muslims, and Christians carry his spiritual seed. He is the trunk of our family tree. His roots run deep in all of us.

Abraham is a man of action. He left Ur, the home of his birth in Mesopotamia. He fought wars, rescued captives, and went to Egypt. He used divide and conquer, surprise, and the dark to overcome great enemies (Gen. 14). When he met the mysterious king of Salem—Melchizedek—he gave away 10 percent of everything he owned (Gen. 14:18–20). He has been blessed, and he is a blessing.

If we are going to change the way we behave for the sake of our children's children, we need to learn from Abraham. Abraham

---

Job, one of the most godly men who ever lived,

"championed the cause of the stranger" (Job 29:16).

believes that God can show up at any time. He believes in the future. Abraham is a planter of trees, a tender of flocks, and a protector of the poor. To rest one's head on the bosom of Abraham is to be in heaven.

Once, in the time long ago before light pollution and smog, God stood outdoors at night with Abraham. A thin, white scimitar shone on the right side of the moon. God put his arm around Abraham and said, *Look at the view Abraham; it is the best view in the galaxy. It is the galaxy!* (Gen. 15:5–6). The Milky Way shone overhead like phosphorescent Queen Anne's lace.

I promise on myself, said the Lord, *that your children will outnumber the stars.*

I make a promise with you, forever, and forever (Gen. 17:7–8). Forever is a long time. Stars are without number. There is a future. The faith of Abraham is a belief in the future even when it seems unlikely or impossible. The trees beat a harmony, the stars cry out in song. God does not meet Abraham in a place that looks like a strip mall. He does not call Abraham on a cell phone or leave a text message.

There are two parts to hospitality: guest and host. Jesus acts as both. He identifies with the stranger:

"I was hungry and you gave me food, I was thirsty and you gave me something to drink, I was a stranger and you welcomed me" (Matt. 25:35),

as well as the host:

"He took a loaf of bread, and when he had given thanks, he broke it and gave it to them, saying, 'This is my body, which is given for you. Do this in remembrance of me.' And he did the same with the cup after supper, saying, 'This cup that is poured out for you is the new covenant in my blood'" (Luke 22:19–20).

By the time the three angels arrive, Sarah and Abraham are well on in years. We could reasonably ask, Why does God pick this old man to be the father of the monotheistic nations of the world? One of the reasons could be that Abraham is green. He is not green just because he and Sarah get their groceries locally—although that matters. Abraham is a man who dwells among trees. He plants trees, and he worships God under them (Gen. 21:33). Over the coming generations, his family will prove themselves worthy of God's trust by:

- Their hospitality
- Their kindness to animals
- Their ability to handle climate change
- Their obedience to God
- Their care of the earth

But in the short run, Sarah gives birth to Isaac. Isaac is most famous for having almost become a human sacrifice. I still remember the first time I heard the story of Isaac in church. I was still in grade school. I didn't like this God who asked Abraham to sacrifice his son. As a young male, I could relate to Isaac—not God. It is unfortunate that the pastor at our small country church did not take time to explain a particular literary devices used in this story—the biblical equivalent of a disclaimer.

Imagine that you are driving down the road listening to the radio. A newscaster is talking about mounting world tensions—the other side

---

Christian hospitality focuses on welcoming not only family and friends into the home, but also strangers.

"When you give a banquet, invite the poor, the crippled, the lame, and the blind. And you will be blessed, because they cannot repay you, for you will be repaid at the resurrection of the righteous" (Luke 14:13–14).

is arming their nuclear rockets. In midsentence the reporter is cut off. Her voice is replaced by the tone of the emergency broadcast system. The 853-hertz tone continues, and when you try another station, it's there, too. EEEEEEEEEEEEEEEEEEEEE!!!!!!!!!!!!!!!!!!!!!!!!!!!!!!!!!!!

Many would start praying or turn around and head for home or try to contact loved ones on their cell phones.

But our response would be completely different if, prior to the emergency tone, the same announcer simply stated: "This is a test of the emergency broadcast system." EEEEEEEEEEEEEEEE-EEEEE!!!!!!!!!!!!!!!!!!!!!!!!!!!!!!!!!!!!!! Under those circumstances, you wouldn't even bother changing the radio station.

The warning makes all the difference. And this is exactly what happens before the story of the binding of Isaac. *"God tested Abraham"* (Gen. 22:1) announces the warning. Before hearing the rest of the events, we know the binding of Isaac is a test. Yet we Christians see the story as a foreshadowing of a real event: the sacrifice of Christ. Sacrifice is the foundation of the Christian faith. The patriarch Abraham puts his home, son, and wealth at the disposal of God, strangers, and kings. His is a "living sacrifice."

During communion, Christians take the host—or the sacrifice—into themselves. We become the host when we sacrifice for others. When we sacrifice, we become more Christlike. This change does not make sense. Graphs cannot define this transformation. Becoming a host is one of the mysteries of the faith. It is.

One of the most significant and pervasive ways that sacrifice is demonstrated throughout the biblical text is the rule, or rather the law, of hospitality. The words *host, hospital, hospice,* and *hospitality* all have the same root: *hostia* equals "sacrifice."

Ultimately, God the Creator and his earth are host to all life.

"[A]ll that is in the heavens and on earth is yours; yours is the kingdom, O Lord, and you are exalted as head above all" (1 Chr. 29:11).

What is the opposite of sacrifice? Greed? Selfishness? Detachment? Gluttony? The Bible suggests that it is also shortsightedness, and lack of concern for others.

After eating at Abraham's home, two of the angels arrive in the nearby Sodom and Gomorrah and are accorded hospitality and protection by Abraham's nephew, Lot. So far, so good. Yet the men of the town want to assault the angels (Gen. 19). The town is vaporized the next day. The saying, "What happens in Sodom and Gomorrah stays in Sodom and Gomorrah" is coined.

Nowhere can the opposite of sacrifice be more readily seen than in the gated twin cities of sin: Sodom and Gomorrah. These towns stand as a direct contrast to the hospitality offered by Abraham. They serve as an example of how *not* to behave toward guests, as does the story of my Kenyan friend who was not offered dinner at her professor's house.

I sometimes wonder what we who believe in religion appear like to those who do not. Nonbelievers must marvel at our endless disagreements on points of theology. I believe that there is no more persuasive evangelism than the theology of an open door, a warm meal, and a bed pulled back for the traveler. When we welcome the stranger into our home, it is as if we are welcoming Jesus. God opens his home, the earth, to us. Each and every one of us is a guest of God, the true owner of everything in heaven and on earth. By sharing his creation with others, we show respect and appreciation for our ultimate Host.

A few months ago, I remarked to my wife, Nancy, that I felt like I had washed a lot of dishes recently. She said that she felt like she had done a lot of cooking. So she counted up all the guests who had sat

---

We, as good guests, are to share this hospitality with all creatures, great and small, for in our host's

"hand is the life of every creature and the breath of all mankind"

(Job 12:10).

at our table in the previous eight days: thirty-eight separate guests, including several who had stayed overnight and shared multiple meals with us.

Today our daughter, Emma, wandered into my home office. A stranger had just shown up at our door. I invited him in and offered him something to eat and drink. "It's funny how I think it's normal to have people I never met show up at the dinner table," she remarked later.

Sometimes Nancy and I think that we have gone too far with hospitality. Lack of privacy, the need for boundaries, setting aside couple time and family time—these are all issues that need to be addressed. Yet the basic premise that our home is not ours but rather a base for missions is central to our creation-care way of life, and a habit that we are proud to have passed along to our children.

God does not want us only to *entertain* people; he wants us to make our home, the earth, a welcome and inviting place for any and all. Hospitality is so much more than changing the sheets and putting out fresh guest towels. Hospitality includes making the air breathable, the water drinkable, and the land arable. It means not closing off our communities through no-trespassing laws and not making our lawns toxic by spraying on chemicals so that insects, birds, dogs, and little children are poisoned when they touch the grass.

Heaven is God's throne, and the earth is his footstool. Because of God's outrageous hospitality, we are welcome to live on his earth. But we are not, through our wasteful and acquisitive practices, supposed to make it an inhospitable place for blue pike, buffalo, and passenger pigeons. We are certainly not called to make the earth,

> *There He was, homeless. Would a church take Him in today—feed Him, clothe Him, offer Him a bed? I hope I ask myself that question on the last day of my life.*
>
> *Dorothy Day (1897–1980)*

our home on loan from God, so inhospitable that it causes the extinction of whole species at the rate of more than twenty thousand
per year, which by conservative estimates is at least one thousand
times the normal background rate of extinction.

"*Keep on loving each other as brothers and sisters. Don't forget to
show hospitality to strangers, for some who have done this have enter-
tained angels without realizing it!*" (Heb. 13:1–2 NLT) One way we
show love to our brothers and sisters is to make the earth, our home,
a clean, green, and welcoming place for all, including all of God's
creatures throughout the world as well as for future generations.

Hospitality, for Paul as for Jesus before him, is not just a practical
issue. It is a fundamental expression of the gospel: a response to
God's hospitality to humankind in providing Christ as the "paschal
lamb" (1 Cor. 5:7) and an outworking of what it means to be members
of the one "body of Christ."

"Hospitality," in Dictionary of the Later New Testament and Its
Developments, S. C. Barton

Tending the Garden
What you can do to show hospitality

- Invite someone new at church over for a meal.
- Bring a loaf of bread to a neighbor who just moved in.
- Plan a communal celebration for Advent, Passover, Succoth, or another lesser-known festival.
- Organize a neighborhood block party.
- Plan a quarterly potluck, with a local-foods theme.
- Offer to share tools and lawn equipment with neighbors.
- Start a share board at church for infrequently used items.
- Join www.freecycle.org to give away items you no longer need.
- Volunteer at a refugee-resettlement ministry.
- Volunteer at a homeless shelter.
- Volunteer at a food pantry or soup kitchen.
- If you own a pickup truck, make others feel welcome to borrow it.
- If you own a canoe, camping gear, or other little-used recreation equipment, offer it to others.
- Call on people who recently lost a loved one, and give your full attention. Listen to their stories, and share their sorrows.
- Start a community garden, and share the produce.
- Become God's networker: introduce a newcomer to friends who share similar interests.
- If possible, set up a guest room in your home where guests can stay comfortably. Make hosting guests a priority in how you use the space in your home.

- Host a creation-care group, book-reading group, faith group, home group, or spiritual group. Make sharing a meal a regular part of the gatherings.

- Share a skill: teach others how to can produce, sew a quilt, knit, dry and preserve fruits, navigate public transportation, repair a bicycle, grow vegetables, read English, dress for a job interview, or bake bread.

- Visit a shut-in. Bring playing cards, a book to read out loud, a game of chess, or a meal to share.

- Invite local college or boarding-school students to share a home-cooked meal in your home.

- Join with others in your church to adopt a refugee family, and help them navigate the resettlement process.

- Consider adoption, foster parenting, or becoming a Big Brother or Big Sister volunteer.

- If you know of a child (materially rich or poor) who would benefit from consistent adult attention, engage in small acts to become an adopted "aunt" or "uncle."

- When someone knocks at the door, stop what you are doing and welcome the person in. Giving your full attention to someone is one of the greatest acts of hospitality.

Adapted with permission from Go Green, Save Green: A Simple Guide to Saving Time, Money and God's Green Earth *(Nancy Sleeth, Tyndale, 2009). For more ideas, visit www.blessedearth.org.*

FOUR

Stewardship
Pharaoh's Dream

After two whole years, Pharaoh dreamed that he was standing
by the Nile, and there came up out of the Nile seven sleek and
fat cows, and they grazed in the reed grass. Then seven other
cows, ugly and thin, came up out of the Nile after them, and
stood by the other cows on the bank of the Nile. The ugly and
thin cows ate up the seven sleek and fat cows. And Pharaoh
awoke. Then he fell asleep and dreamed a second time; seven
ears of grain, plump and good, were growing on one stalk. Then
seven ears, thin and blighted by the east wind, sprouted after
them. The thin ears swallowed up the seven plump and full
ears. Pharaoh awoke, and it was a dream. In the morning his
spirit was troubled; so he sent and called for all the magicians
of Egypt and all its wise men. Pharaoh told them his dreams,
but there was no one who could interpret them to Pharaoh.

(Gen. 41:1–8)

Recently I was sitting in the office of the vice president of a large
seminary. I have great respect for this man and the institution he
represents, so when he asks me a question, I take it seriously.

"Matthew," he said, "from a creation-care point of view, which do
you think is better—coal or nuclear energy?"

"Good question." I paused to collect my thoughts. I wanted
my answer to be both biblical and logical. "Let's take nuclear first.

Although nuclear has a pretty good track record worldwide, we've also had Chernobyl and Three Mile Island to learn from. Another problem is that we don't have a good plan for dealing with nuclear waste in the United States. We also have to consider the mining of uranium itself, which has some pretty significant environmental effects. Arsenic, lead, cadmium, and other harmful heavy metals tend to hang out with uranium in rocks, so nuclear leads to some serious water-pollution problems. But perhaps the most worrisome issue with uranium and nuclear technology is its potential to be used for terrorism or as a weapon."

I paused to see if the seminary VP was following me. He nodded for me to go on.

"But coal also has its problems, starting with how it's extracted. Strip-mining and mountaintop removal are responsible for destroying vast ecosystems. Once we get the coal out of the ground, there's the problem of slurry and slag lakes, a number of which have collapsed in recent years and flooded entire towns. After we get the coal to the plant, there's the problem of air pollution. Coal-fired plants are the biggest source of mercury in the environment and contribute significant amounts of CO_2 to the air. They also add a lot of particulate matter, which aggravates asthma and respiratory diseases. It's been estimated that each coal-fired plant contributes to one hundred and twenty deaths in the United States every year."

I took a slow sip from my glass of water before launching into my alternative proposal. "When the city of Austin, Texas, was faced with the need to build a new power plant, they took a different approach: conservation. Instead of going with coal or nuclear, the city built what they call an 'energy conservation power plant.' Through

---

God created the earth, and it belongs to him.

"The earth is the Lord's and all that is in it, the world, and those who live in it; for he has founded it on the seas, and established it on the rivers" (Ps. 24:1–2).

conservation, the community was able to continue to grow without generating more power. After twenty years, Austin now saves more than six hundred megawatts of electricity every day—one power plant worth of electricity generated strictly from energy savings.

"For me, the bottom line is, which would I rather have in my backyard: a coal plant or a nuclear plant? That's like being asked if I'd rather be hit with a brick or a baseball bat.

"Truth be told, I'd rather have a chocolate-chip cookie."

The seminary leader laughed, so I didn't need to spell out the obvious: conservation is the best answer. Austin's example provides a doable vision that can be achieved on any scale, in any community in America that makes conservation a priority, beginning today. An individual can build a tiny conservation power plant in his or her home by changing lightbulbs and hanging clothes on the line. A business, school, or church can do the same on a larger scale by investing in an energy audit and performance contractor. An entire city or municipal utility can go even further and commit to a program on the scale of Austin.

To illustrate why conservation is not only the logical course but a scriptural one as well, let's look at the story of Joseph in Exodus. Joseph's interpretation of the first recorded environmental dream is more relevant today than ever.

The story centers on a guy named Joe, the great-grandson of our friend Abe. Joe comes from a blended family. His dad, Jacob, has fathered children by four women. Joe's biological mom is a thief, and he himself is doing hard time in a Memphis prison. He was convicted of assault and attempted rape. Although Joe claims to be innocent, fabric evidence from a piece of Joe's clothing places him

---

God entrusted his creation to our care.

"Think of us in this way, as servants of Christ and stewards of God's mysteries. Moreover, it is required of stewards that they be found trustworthy" (1 Cor. 4:1–2).

at the crime scene. It appears that Joseph will end his days in jail, but God has other plans. Joseph is given a position of responsibility within the prison. When Pharaoh's cupbearer and baker are thrown in jail and have disturbing dreams, they turn to Joseph for help. Joseph accurately interprets the dreams, and the cupbearer promises to help Joseph in return.

As predicted, three days later the cupbearer is released from prison, but his promises to Joseph are immediately forgotten. Joseph appears to be stuck in the slammer for eternity, but God—who has a different sense of time than we do—has not forgotten Joseph.

One night Pharaoh wakes with a start and glances across the shoulder of his wife. The alarm clock reads 3:34. He has just had the strangest dream. It is about cows. He reaches for the last of his drink on the nightstand, drains it, and drifts back to sleep. He dreams again, this time about corn. In the morning he wakes with a hangover and a troubled mind. He wants answers. What do these dreams mean?

Pharaoh sends for the most renowned experts. Tenured dream interpreters arrive in a whirl of chariots. They roll out scrolls filled with dreams about going to class and forgetting to study and going to work and forgetting to dress. They pour through dreams of flying and dreams of being chased through the mazes of pyramids. They read dreams about wandering through palaces and temples. But they cannot find a single mad-cow dream. Nowhere in the database does anyone come across fat cows being devoured by skinny, carnivorous

---

A good conservationist learns to use, but not abuse, God's creation.

"If you come on a bird's nest, in any tree or on the ground, with fledglings or eggs, with the mother sitting on the fledglings or on the eggs, you shall not take the mother with the young. Let the mother go, taking only the young for yourself, in order that it may go well with you and you may live long" (Deut. 22:6–7).

ones. Who will interpret these strange dreams? What do they mean for the market, the GNP, and national security? The palace is in an uproar.

Finally, the cupbearer slaps himself on the forehead, "Joseph! How could I have forgotten Joseph?"

The cupbearer clears his throat and then addresses Pharaoh: "When I was in prison, the baker and I had dreams on the same night. A fellow prisoner named Joseph was known to be wise, so we asked him the meaning of our dreams. He consulted his God, who said that my dream foretold I would be released in three days and have my job reinstated. And so it came to be."

The cupbearer looks at Pharaoh for a sign. Pharaoh nods. The cupbearer continues, "Joseph's interpretation of the baker's dream was not so happy. The baker's dream meant that in three days he would be tortured and killed. That, too, came true."

Pharaoh does not hesitate. "Send for the prisoner named Joseph. Perhaps his God knows the meaning of my dreams."

What happens next is one of the greatest rags-to-riches stories ever told. Joseph has fallen lower than the ocean floor. He is a forgotten nobody. Once he was loved and had the best of everything, but now:

- He has lost his mother.
- He believes he will never see his father again.
- His brothers have betrayed him.

We are to care for God's creation, even in times of war.

"If you besiege a town for a long time, making war against it in order to take it, you must not destroy its trees by wielding an ax against them. Although you may take food from them, you must not cut them down. Are trees in the field human beings that they should come under siege from you?" (Deut. 20:19).

- He has lost his home and every possession.
- He has been sold into slavery.
- He has been falsely accused of a felony.
- He has been thrown in prison.
- He has been promised help by a man who immediately forgot him.

Then it happens. Just when all hope is lost, a motorcade is sent racing to the prison. Joseph is whisked into the palace, given a shower and shave, and brought into the throne room.

The Pharaoh addresses the prisoner: "You are summoned here today because I have been told that you can interpret dreams."

"I cannot, but my God can," the Hebrew replies.

Then Pharaoh tells Joseph his dream. How I would love to have been there when the king of Egypt finished talking and every eye turned to the man from the prison. Silence, just like in the old ads—*When E. F. Hutton talks, people listen.*

Joseph's answer is not what anyone expects, least of all the ruler of this prosperous nation. It is not an answer Pharaoh wants to hear, and yet it is the truth, given to Joseph by God: "You will have seven good years." A collective sigh of relief.

Poor stewardship and conservation practices have consequences for humanity and the earth.

*"Ah, you who join house to house, who add field to field, until there is room for no one but you, and you are left to live alone in the midst of the land! The L*ORD *of hosts has sworn in my hearing: Surely many houses shall be desolate, large and beautiful houses, without inhabitant.*

For ten acres of vineyard shall yield but one bath, and a homer of seed shall yield a mere ephah" (Isa. 5:8–10).

The prisoner continues, "And then the climate will change, and you will have seven years so harsh that you will forget there ever was a good time."

"What would you have us do?" the king of Egypt inquires.

"Conserve," Joseph says.

"Define *conserve*."

The chief librarian from Alexandria rolls open the *Oxford English Dictionary*. She looks down the scroll and reads:

"'Conserve, to keep from harm, decay, loss, or waste, especially with a view to later use; preserve with care.'"

"Ah, to care for the future," repeats Pharaoh. "To conserve, to preserve. Yes, that is the Egyptian way."

Through Joseph, the Pharaoh hears the voice of God—and listens to reason.

"What should I do to take us through the seven lean years that you predict?"

"Place a reasonable person in charge," Joseph replied. "Then enact a 20 percent tax on all harvests from the bounty of the next seven years. Store up the food collected from this tax and protect it in central locations. When the time of the great famine arrives, this food will save the land of Egypt" (see Gen. 41:33–36).

Joseph didn't say, "Let's appoint a committee to study this issue," or "let's start drilling under the pyramids for water," or "I'm sure the scientists and wise men will come up with some technology to save us." What he said was, "Let's become conservationists. Let's conserve."

We will be blessed if we care for God's creation, but cursed if we don't.

"You shall keep my statutes and my ordinances and commit none of these abominations . . . otherwise the land will vomit you out for defiling it, as it vomited out the nation that was before you" (Lev. 18:26, 28).

Joseph's prediction was especially astounding because of the regularity of the flood and the almost nonexistent phenomenon of seven consecutive years without flooding. However, it is clear from archeological evidence that there was, in fact, a period of vast hunger in the land of Egypt during the time of Joseph. Even with the 20 percent conservation tax, it would have been difficult to survive the seven lean years.

It is even possible that Joseph and his call to conservation put Egypt back on the track of reliable central government—without which Egypt and its surrounding neighbors would have suffered much more severely during the time of famine. Further, Joseph paved the way for his father, his brothers, and their families to become shareholders in the rich land of Goshen. During the Hebrews' 430-year stay in Egypt, Jacob's descendants grew from a family to a nation.

Pharaoh's dream and Joseph's God-inspired conservation plan made it possible for Egypt to get through the lean times and flourish—a biblical precedent for how we should respond to environmental degradation and declining natural resources today.

Both personally and corporately, our culture has been raised to believe that the good times will roll forever. The Bible and history teach us that life moves in cycles. Preparation for the downturns is best made during the up cycles. Although we may have little control over the broad and varied society in which we live, we have a majority vote over the constitution of our own souls, our behaviors, and our homes.

Those who do not conserve God's creation will suffer severe penalties.

"The nations raged, but your wrath has come, and the time for judging the dead, for rewarding your servants, the prophets and saints and all who fear your name, both small and great, and for destroying those who destroy the earth" (Rev. 11:18).

Environmental topics can get so politicized and polarizing that we absolve ourselves from personal responsibility. People on both sides of the issue argue with great passion. In their heart of hearts, they hold their opinions as moral bedrock and doubt the sanity of their opponents. Yet, if the truth were told, we'd discover that many who hold diametrically opposed opinions about the environment go home to lives that are indistinguishable from one another's.

The Bible is filled with passionate people—the most amazing array of dysfunctional characters that can be imagined. In short, it is filled with people like you and me. Studying the triumphs and pitfalls of the flawed lives described within its pages gives us powerful tools for personal insight and wisdom.

For example, thinking about Joseph and Pharaoh, we can ask ourselves:

If I had been present when Joseph predicted hard times ahead, what would have been my reaction?

Would I have said it can't be true, because the Nile is so regular in its cycle of flooding?

Would I have doubted the messenger because he was from another social class or practiced a different religion?

What would be the harm that could come from following Joseph's advice—or ignoring it?

Would I have followed his plan because it seemed the logical thing to do or because he spoke as a messenger of the Lord?

Because God gives us free will, we can choose stewardship or selfishness, conservation or consumption, redemption or destruction. God wants us to choose life.

"I have set before you life and death, blessings and curses. Choose life so that you and your descendants may live, loving the LORD your God, obeying him, and holding fast to him" (Deut. 30:19–20).

Is it not possible that logic, prudence, and conservation are the course that God would have us take?

If we can learn from biblical history, perhaps we also can start learning from the mistakes of recent history. Again, we need to ask ourselves how we would have reacted, with limited knowledge and an unknown future:

How would I have come down on requiring catalytic converters in automobiles?

Would I have been for or against removing lead from gasoline, paints, and toys?

Would I have just talked, argued, and worried about these things—or would I have taken personal steps to mitigate the effect of harmful toxins, when I could?

Would I have said, "It's not my problem," or would I have worried more about its effect on my neighbor?

Would I have settled for short-term "solutions" or been more concerned about my great-grandchildren's lives?

As we learn from the mistakes we have made, we can begin to see them as the gifts they are: the keys to a better future. If I can't remember the last time I was wrong on an issue, I'm not thinking biblically. The Bible is a kind of master key: when used in wisdom, it allows us to avoid repeating mistakes and some of the outcomes of poor choices.

> *It is not right for us to destroy the world God has given us. . . . To drive to extinction something He has created is wrong. He has a purpose for everything. . . . We Christians have a responsibility to take the lead in caring for the earth.*
>
> Detroit Free Press, *Billy Graham (1918–)*

This strategy—turning to the Bible for answers and learning from past mistakes—is central to the conservation message. When sitting in the seminary office, I told my brother in Christ that I do not know with complete certainty which is worse: coal or nuclear. I can say, however, with 100 percent certainty that when I go into any large city and see a dome of smog hanging over it, I know that it is caused by our cars, factories, and houses. I know that industrial pollutants make children get sick and die. I know with all my heart that God did not intend fish to be tainted with dioxin and mercury or the roots of trees to sicken because of acid rain.

The French philosopher Blaise Pascal wrote a collection of thoughts that were published after his death. *Pensees* has 924 of his musings. By far the most well known is number 233, also known as *Pascal's Gambit* or *Pascal's Wager.* His original discussion focuses on the probability of the existence of an infinite God; Pascal's logic also can be applied to environmental issues.

If we believe in God and God turns out not to exist, then we have lost very little by our wager (belief). If, on the other hand, we do not believe in God and God does exist, then we have lost eternity/infinity.

When applied to the environment, the reasoning goes something like this: If we clean up the air and retool our country for renewable energy and the environmental disasters that have been predicted don't happen, we lose nothing and still gain much. If we continue business as usual and the predicted environmental disasters do occur, unprecedented numbers of people will die because of droughts, floods, and lack of access to clean water, soil, and air.

> *The custody of the garden was given to Adam, to show that we possess the things which God has committed to our hands, on the condition that, being content with the frugal and moderate use of them, we should take care of what shall remain.*
> Commentary on Genesis, *John Calvin (1509–1564)*

By making simple changes around the house, my family and I were able to reduce our electricity use by nine-tenths and our fossil-fuel use by two-thirds. Using compact fluorescent lightbulbs, adding insulation, drying clothes on the line, and adjusting the thermostat all add up to big savings. In essence, our home became a miniature Austin—an energy conservation power plant. These changes were motivated by common sense, by our faith, and by our belief that the Bible holds answers to all of today's problems, including environmental issues.

As a former ER doctor, I believe the wager to clean up the air and build sustainable infrastructures is like having a seatbelt and airbag in your car. Better to have one and not need it than to need one and not have it.

Even more important, changing our consumption habits allowed my family to demonstrate greater respect for God's creation and love for our neighbors The biblical lesson of Pharaoh's dream corresponds with Pascal's logic: we must tamp down our hubris, learn from past mistakes, and begin to conserve God's resources.

Conservation makes biblical sense. Conservation makes common sense. As a man of faith and a man of science, I endorse conservation as the *first* place to take action.

The expression, "I own something and have more than enough; why should I not enjoy it?" is not worthy of man nor does it indicate any community feeling. The alternative expression however does: "I have something, why should I not share it with those in need?" Such a one is on the right path, and fulfills the command: Thou shalt love thy neighbor as thyself.

Christ the Educator, *St. Clement of Alexandria (c. 150–c. 215)*

Tending the Garden
What you can do to conserve energy

- Ask your local utility to conduct an energy audit on your home and/or business, and then heed their advice.

- Turn thermostats up three degrees (in summer) and down three degrees (in winter).

- Always turn off lights, TV, radio, and stereo when leaving the room.

- Replace lightbulbs with compact fluorescent bulbs.

- Unplug TV and stereo when not in use or put them on a switched power strip to avoid "phantom loads."

- When replacing appliances, purchase the most efficient (Energy Star), with the lowest yearly energy costs.

- Visit the grocery only once each week. Combine trips. Carpool.

- Air-dry laundry.

- Caulk and weather-strip around windows and doors to plug air leaks.

- Stock up on handkerchiefs, cloth shopping bags, and cloth napkins. Avoid purchasing anything with the word *disposable*.

- Wait a month before buying something you "need"; when you do make purchases, buy quality items that will last for many years.

- When replacing a car, consider a hybrid or one that gets great mileage and has low emissions.

- Hang thick or insulated curtains. Close them during the day in summer; close at night in winter.

- Vacation closer to home.

- Avoid covering radiators and vents with furniture or curtains; program thermostats to come on thirty minutes before waking up or coming home.

- Insulate your attic with a minimum of fourteen inches of insulation; insulate your hot-water heater if it's an older model.

- Insulate your hot-water pipes; it's easy—just slip on the foam insulation.

- Turn down the temperature on your hot-water heater to a lower setting.

- Cut food before cooking; put the lid on pans; cook outside in summer.

- Reduce the amount of junk mail you receive by registering at www.dmaconsumers.org/cgi/offmailinglist.

- Ask God to help you become a better steward of his resources.

- Follow our grandmothers' advice: "Use it up, wear it out, make it do, or do without."

Adapted with permission from Go Green, Save Green: A Simple Guide to Saving Time, Money and God's Green Earth *(Nancy Sleeth, Tyndale, 2009). For more ideas, visit www.blessedearth.org.*

FIVE

Work and Rest

Exodus from Slavery

On the sixth day they gathered twice as much food, two omers apiece. When all the leaders of the congregation came and told Moses, he said to them, "This is what the Lord has commanded: 'Tomorrow is a day of solemn rest, a holy sabbath to the Lord; bake what you want to bake and boil what you want to boil, and all that is left over put aside to be kept until morning.'" So they put it aside until morning, as Moses commanded them; and it did not become foul, and there were no worms in it. Moses said, "Eat it today, for today is a sabbath to the Lord; today you will not find it in the field. Six days you shall gather it; but on the seventh day, which is a sabbath, there will be none." On the seventh day some of the people went out to gather, and they found none. The Lord said to Moses, "How long will you refuse to keep my commandments and instructions? See! The Lord has given you the sabbath, therefore on the sixth day he gives you food for two days; each of you stay where you are; do not leave your place on the seventh day." So the people rested on the seventh day. *(Exod. 16:22–30)*

Years ago, I started taking a day off work every week. I did this religiously—even before I believed in God. I started this practice because I was getting older and it was getting harder for me to work long shifts in the emergency department—particularly night shifts.

My decision turned out to be life-transforming, though at the time it was merely a survival technique.

On my weekly "stop day" I would not work, do chores, or go shopping. I spent the time reading books or listening to taped lectures about history and philosophy. I took naps in the middle of the day. I went for walks with Nancy or the kids. I chilled.

One particular fall evening defines "stop day" for me. Our children, Emma and Clark, and I were in the attic of our old house, a large, nearly empty room with windows at either end and a hammock set up under the rafters. The temperature outside had dropped, but inside the attic remained comfortably warm. I was reading a book to the kids in the hammock, while Clark tugged rhythmically at the pull rope. The pull rope worked independently of the hammock's suspension system, allowing us to rock gently and consistently without touching the floor. Emma's head of blond curls was snuggled up on my left shoulder, while Clark's rested on the other.

I finished reading the book, set it on the floor, and put my newly freed arms around them both. The hammock swayed back and forth, counting each moment, like a pendulum.

Emma fell asleep. Then Clark drifted off. The hammock slowed. Each child had a hand resting on my chest. Somewhere in their slumber, they felt reassured by my breathing, my heartbeat, and my warm presence—just as I was calmed by theirs.

Time stopped.

I do not know how long we lay there. It grew dark and still. Nancy eventually came with a flashlight and carried Emma to bed while I carried Clark.

God set the pattern for humanity: work six days and rest the seventh.

"On the seventh day God finished the work that he had done, and he rested on the seventh day from all the work that he had done" (Gen. 2:2).

That hammock time will always define *Shabbat Shalom* for me: "Stop, and know peace."

When our entire family became followers of Christ, we continued a stop day. It became a sacred time. My children would get their homework done the night before. We looked forward to Shabbat peace all week.

One of the immediate effects of coming to rest one day a week was a 10 to 14 percent reduction in our transportation and consumer consumption; moreover, this weekly rest allowed us to resist the incessant call for consumerism on the other six days. Some experts estimate that we view as many as *thirty thousand media messages per day*. A Sabbath way of life is all about self-restraint and being content with enough. I believe that remembering the Sabbath is perhaps the single most important factor in our family's coming together to pursue a less materialistic, more spiritual life of conservation and stewardship.

Jews describe stop day as a bride. It is a beautiful experience for which we all long. It is a honeymoon from time. On a wedding night, one does not worry about the stock market, pollution, or housework. Stop days are intimate, sensual, and guiltless. They should be jealously guarded.

I wrote about stop days in *Serve God, Save the Planet*. After the book was published, I continued to practice a lifestyle of conservation. But the pace of my life changed. I began to speak on Saturdays and Sundays. Then I was lecturing during the week. Sometimes I would be in a place for one or two weeks at a time. The churches I was speaking at got bigger. Sometimes they would have a Saturday evening service and three or four Sunday services. Last year I was on

---

The seventh day is a time of holy rest.

"God blessed the seventh day and hallowed it, because on it God rested from all the work that he had done in creation" (Gen. 2:3).

the road for 230 days. Somewhere along the way I stopped taking a day off every week. Life got hectic, and there no longer seemed to be enough time.

My crazy pace of life was not unique; the mantra of today is "I'm too busy." Because we've become so obsessed with time, we fill our world with time-keeping devices. We have clocks on the computer, wall, dashboard, billboard, bank sign, DVD/CD/MP3 player, TV, VCR, PlayStation, Xbox, camera, camcorder, microwave, bread maker, oven, radio, paperweight, GPS, coffeemaker, pacemaker, PalmPilot, taxi, plane, truck, tractor, airport, boat, surveillance camera, cash register, pedometer, scoreboard, defibrillator, space station, missile, and egg timer. There is a clock on my wrist and one in the tower two blocks from my house. There's one beside my bed and one on the telephone. Clocks are everywhere; the world is filled with billions of them.

Even children are not immune. Toddlers wake up to alarm clocks so they can get to preschool on time. These little ones emerge from the simple world of waking and napping into a world divided and ruled by hours, minutes, and seconds. Preschoolers are given board books where they learn to spin the hour and minute hands, as if humans—not God—controlled the celestial movements.

Our chronographs run on sun, sand, springs, and electricity. To define intervals of time, they use pendulums, gears, quartz, cesium, and strontium. The most primitive will not operate if a cloud passes by, and the most accurate will not gain a second in two hundred million years.

We watch, punch, cheat, and try to beat the clock. *Just a second. Wait a minute.* Catch up, hurry up, and make up time. The problem

---

This shared pattern of work and rest is a tie that binds humankind to God, and God to humankind.

"Hallow my sabbaths that they may be a sign between me and you, so that you may know that I the LORD am your God" (Ezek. 20:20).

with instant results is they take too long. *I don't have a minute to spare.*

In our haste to beat the clock, we are not content to do one thing at a time. We multitask. It's nothing to microwave a meal, shop online, and sip a soda simultaneously. We drink instant coffee while we drive, drive while we answer the phone, and phone while we walk. *Can you hold that thought for a moment while I get this other call?*

Our culture is described as being 24/7. There is a loneliness and desperation that accompanies such busy lives. We are slaves to the clock. Not only is the 24/7 life unhealthy for humans—it's bad for creation. What are the implications of 24/7 mining, marketing, fishing, building, and paving? What does Scripture say about people trapped in a 24/7 life?

A lot. Let's open the Bible to the book of Exodus. A brutal pharaoh, Ramses, is now in power. He believes that the Hebrew people have become too numerous and too powerful, so he orders the midwives to kill all the newborn boys. The midwives refuse, saying the Hebrew women deliver their babies too fast. When medical right-sizing fails, Ramses tries Plan B, commanding "all his people" to go in search of and kill newborn male Hebrews. This orgy of child killing has its consequences. The entire Egyptian people have blood on their hands.

In this setting of despair, one slave couple marries, conceives, and gives birth to a baby boy. Like an ancient Anne Frank, this child is hidden from the authorities until he becomes too old to conceal. The mother hatches a daring plan to save his life; she puts him in a tiny ark set adrift on the Nile. The lifeboat is found. Pharaoh's daughter takes pity on the baby, adopts him, and names him Moses.

> **Those who keep the Sabbath will be rewarded abundantly.**
>
> *"All who keep the sabbath, and do not profane it, and hold fast my covenant—these I will bring to my holy mountain, and make them joyful in my house of prayer" (Isa. 56:6–7).*

Moses grows up in the luxury of the palace while his Hebrew people toil under conditions that go from bad to desperate. He learns to read, write, and fight. Somehow he also hears of his Hebrew heritage. What must it have been like to take the weekend off while his people made bricks, day after day, under horrific conditions?

After seeing a Hebrew slave brutally beaten, something in Moses snaps, and he kills one of the taskmasters. Moses is forced to flee to the land of Midian. There, he comes upon a group of shepherdesses out tending their flock. The women's access to the well is blocked by a group of aggressive men. Moses drives the men from the area and waters the flock himself.

Watering the animals is a curious detail in the story, but it should not be dismissed as trivial. Compassion for beasts of the field is a recurring biblical theme. Animals, like people, need respite and rest. Once again, concern for all of God's creatures is practiced by a player on God's redemption team. Consider that Moses is a prince and has probably never even stabled his own horse. Watering sheep is not an act to gain the women's attention or sympathy. An Egyptian prince stopping to water the flock would be like the vice president stopping on the Beltway to change a stranger's flat tire. Moses performs this service as an affirmation of his character. Can you picture Ramses stooping to water goats or sheep?

In the book of Leviticus and elsewhere in the Torah, Moses communicates God's "operating instructions" for the proper care of livestock, wildlife, and land. These rules include giving the land a rest every seven years. Even beasts of the field should be given a Sabbath rest. The Hebrew people have not owned real estate before. God shows them how to care for the land he gives them, not only

---

Sabbath rest is a gift that should be treasured.

"[Jesus] said to them, 'The sabbath was made for humankind, and not humankind for the Sabbath'" (Mark 2:27).

to ensure their personal health and well-being, but so the land can benefit the stranger, orphan, widow, and future generations—that is, the friendless and the landless.

We have seen that God approves of those who care for the land and for helpless animals, but is it wrong to mistreat them—for example, to work the beasts of the field to exhaustion? In modern terms, does *not* giving the land or animals a rest have a negative predictive consequence in the Bible?

One example of negative treatment can be found in the closing chapters of Genesis. Here a blessing is delivered over two of Joseph's brothers, Simeon and Levi. These are the same brothers who threw Joseph in the well and intended to kill him. These are not blessings in the same way that we use the term today. A better definition would be "God's judgments."

> Simeon and Levi are two of a kind;
> their weapons are instruments of violence.
> May I never join in their meetings;
> may I never be a party to their plans.
> For in their anger they murdered men,
> and they crippled oxen just for sport.
> A curse on their anger, for it is fierce;
> a curse on their wrath, for it is cruel. *(Gen. 49:5–7, NLT)*

"You are violent, you are cruel to animals, get out of my face." That's what God thinks of these two brothers.

The Sabbath is a gift that cannot be rescinded, a permanent blessing that ties us to God.

"So then, a sabbath rest still remains for the people of God; for those who enter God's rest also cease from their labors as God did from his" (Heb. 4:9–10).

God hears the groaning of the Israelites in Egypt, and he calls to Moses from the famous burning bush. "My people are slaves," God tells Moses, "and you and I are going to get them out." Moses returns to Egypt with his brother, Aaron. First, he goes to the Israelite slaves to assure them that God will redeem them. Next stop: Pharaoh's palace.

"Let my people go for a three-day weekend to worship our God," Moses demands. Initially, he's not asking for the Israelites' freedom—just a long weekend to rest and worship. Pharaoh's response is, "I don't know your God, and I don't care. You slaves are going to have to work harder now. I will make you gather your own straw to make the bricks, and not decrease the quota." This is a classic tyrannical management tool: "When the workers ask for a break, speed up the assembly line."

What follows is a back and forth between "I AM THAT I AM" (the God of the Hebrews) and "I'LL DO WHAT I WANT" (the pharaoh of Egypt). Each time God says, "Let my people go!" the pharaoh says, "No." Pharaoh's stubbornness results in ten plagues, culminating on Passover night, when death comes to the firstborn in the households of Egypt. God is punishing the Egyptians for the slaughter of innocent Hebrew newborns and four hundred years of 24/7 enslavement.

Finally, Pharaoh relents. Moses leads the nation of slaves out of Egypt. Moses cannot take the northern route because of the fortifications the Egyptians have installed there. Instead, he heads south-

---

Observing the Sabbath will bring us delight like none other.

"If you refrain from trampling the sabbath, from pursuing your own interests on my holy day; if you call the sabbath a delight and the holy day of the LORD honorable; if you honor it, not going your own ways, serving your own interests, or pursuing your own affairs; then you shall take delight in the LORD, and I will make you ride upon the heights of the earth" (Isa. 58:13–14).

west toward the Red Sea. Pharaoh changes his mind—he wants the slaves back—and the Egyptians give chase to the Israelites. Trapped at the edge of the Red Sea, Moses raises his wooden shepherd's staff, and God parts the waters. The slaves march across on the seabed with Pharaoh and his charioteers in hot pursuit. The charioteers are a seemingly invincible force. They are the equivalent to today's helicopter gunships.

On the one side of the Red Sea is a group of tattered dirty slaves, and on the other side are the builders of pyramids and rulers of slaves. The Egyptians represent a 24/7 life and the "things of this world." God parts the water of the sea, the slaves escape, and God uses the sea to blot out the Egyptian army. This mass drowning held special significance to ancient Egyptians. It represented the defeat of an entire army and the loss of the body of their commander in chief, the pharaoh. In ancient Egyptian thinking, you could not cross to the afterlife without an embalmed body. The loss of a cadaver was the most tragic type of death, a fate worse than death—which is why the baker's fate (hung by a pole so the bird could eat his flesh) was so damning (Gen. 40:18–22).

The Red Sea mass drowning also sets up a clear dichotomy between how God wages war and how humanity wages war. Mankind uses machines, engineering, and forged metal to make statements. God uses wind, water, a bush, a stick, gnats, frogs, the sun—in short, the earth—to get the job done. However, when it comes to giving his ten commandments, God compromises. He carves his instructions in stone (twice)—something he never did before, or since.

God meets this nascent nation in a very human way. These people have lived for centuries with unrelenting work and no rest. Bricks, bricks, bricks is all they understand. They are beaten down

---

The Sabbath is a reminder that all of "our" time belongs to God, not just on the Sabbath, but every day throughout our lives.

"My times are in your hands" (Ps. 31:15).

and subjugated. They have had no time to be still and know God. Therefore, God gives them a physical tablet that they can hold and review at sacred times.

Moses carries the tablets containing "the law." We know this law as the Ten Commandments. The fourth commandment is the longest:

> Remember the sabbath day, to keep it holy. Six days shalt thou labour, and do all thy work: But the seventh day is the sabbath of the LORD thy God: in it thou shalt not do any work, thou, nor thy son, nor thy daughter, thy manservant, nor thy maidservant, nor thy cattle, nor thy stranger that is within thy gates: For in six days the LORD made heaven and earth, the sea, and all that in them is, and rested the seventh day: wherefore the LORD blessed the sabbath day, and hallowed it. *(Exod. 20:8–11, KJV)*

Unlike most of the commandments that begin with "Do not" or "Thou shalt not," this commandment begins with the word "Remember." It is as if God knew that even though the people had been freed from bondage, they would forget to stop working.

When I give a talk at a church, someone invariably will ask, "What is the first thing that I should do to become a better steward of the earth?" This is a great question. I used to answer, "Go home and replace all your lightbulbs with efficient ones." As a Christian, I like the symbolism of beginning a change with light. Changing lightbulbs is low-hanging fruit in the conservation world. However, I have come to believe that one of the greatest things that we have to offer to a dying planet is the fourth commandment. STOP. *"Be still, and know that I am God!"* (Ps. 46:10).

The Sabbath is a time to lay down our burdens and find peace.

"Come to me, all you that are weary and are carrying heavy burdens, and I will give you rest" (Matt. 11:28).

Eden was a place where we were not separated from God. We worked and grew tired—but never weary. Genesis tells of the making of the heavens and the earth, of the animals and fish, and of things that creep, and things that fly. On the seventh day, Scripture tells us, *"God finished the work that he had done, and he rested on the seventh day from all the work that he had done. So God blessed the seventh day and hallowed it, because on it God rested from all the work that he had done in creation"* (Gen. 2:2–3).

Over the millennia, scholars have discussed what God was finishing on the morning of the seventh day. Most agree that he was making *rest*. God created what has been described as "a temple in time."

Just as the Egyptians had no word for *freedom*, the ancient Hebrews had no names for the days. The current pagan names Saturday (Saturn's day), Sunday (the Sun's day), Monday (the Moon's day), Tuesday (Tiwes, the god of war's day), etc., were not in use by the Hebrew people. Instead, they counted the days as one-day, two-day, three-day, four-day, five-day, six-day, "stop day." Stop/rest translates to *Shabbat*, which translates to "Sabbath." Some people believe that stop day is Saturday, some Sunday. No matter what day, I do know this: we should stop one day a week to allow ourselves, and God's creation, to come to rest.

Christ defined the intent of the day of rest, explaining that it is made for the benefit of mankind (Mark 2:27).

The benefits of stopping weekly would be greatest if all on the planet shared a single day. But since that seems unlikely to happen in the near future, let us be thankful it has been narrowed down to either Saturday or Sunday. The question is not so much, Which day to stop? but, Will we stop at all? As I have said, the fourth commandment is

---

Blessed be to God for the day of rest and religious occupation wherein earthly things assume their true size.

Journal, *William Wilberforce (1759–1833)*

longer than any other commandment, and longer than the next six combined. We, like the Israelites, tend to understand the short commandments and ignore or forget the long ones.

On stop day, Jesus picks grain for his disciples and heals the withered hand of the man in the synagogue. He distinguishes between the sacredness of a day of rest and worshiping a day of rest. Yet, "as was his custom," he honors the day. He does not go to the mall, cheer for the gladiators at the pagan sports stadium, or mow the grass. It is a holy day. We can infer by his "labors" on the Sabbath his meaning of the day. The Sabbath is for healing. It is a time to seek still waters and quiet pastures.

Although we are not slaves chained together under the tropical sun, we have retained the mind-set of slaves. The slaves in Egypt didn't have the option of a day of rest, and yet we've rejected it. We are caught in a 24/7 world.

When Nancy first started teaching English, she had a student named Clinton. On the first day of class, she asked students to write an autobiographical essay. Clinton's essay was three pages long. Nancy showed it to me. It had no commas, dashes, periods, or semicolons. It had no paragraph indentations. It was one long, unpunctuated, formless ramble. God did not intend our lives to be like Clinton's paper. Life is not supposed to be a seventy-year run-on sentence.

Musicians have a saying: "It is not the notes that make music; it is the pauses in between." With a weekly day of rest, God ordained and commanded a meter and a rhythm to our lives. He wants us to make music—not noise.

The fourth commandment applies not only to our own lives but to the lives of our "manservants" and "maidservant"—today's

---

I feel as if God had, by giving the Sabbath, given fifty-two springs in every year.

                             Samuel Taylor Coleridge (1772–1834)

minimum-wage workers. This commandment protects the stranger in the land—our illegal aliens—who often work two or three jobs, seven days a week. The Shabbat laws also apply to the animals and provide protection for the land and wildlife.

It is difficult to imagine caring for God's creation or loving our neighbors as ourselves if we do not know how to care for ourselves. We can start doing both by obeying the longest of the commandments.

Last fall I was home for a few days. I wasn't feeling good about life or preaching or much of anything else. Life was too busy. You have all been there. What had gone wrong? I couldn't put my finger on it. Then the mail arrived. I received a letter from a pastor who had seen an article of mine, and he'd written to encourage me. He and his wife were praying for our family. At the end—almost as a postscript—he asked, "Are you taking a Sabbath day weekly?"

I stopped working and just sat there. The phone rang. It was another pastor. We asked about each other's families, and then he brought up the topic of Sabbath rest. In fact, that's why he'd called.

"I've always taken Fridays off," he explained, "because I preach on Sundays and Wednesdays. But after hearing you speak about Sabbath practices, I began to make it a holy day." He went on to tell me some of the routines he'd instituted, like a long walk in silence with his wife, not wearing a watch for the day, and unplugging the computer and TV. "I've been depressed for the last twenty years, and it's finally lifted. I just want to thank you for coming to our church and preaching about this. And to thank you for setting an example."

Busted. God had sent these messengers to heap on much-needed coals of shame. After nearly ten years of honoring the Sabbath, I had started to ignore the fourth commandment.

> *As we keep or break the Sabbath day, we nobly save or meanly lose the last and best hope by which man arises.*
>
> *Speech delivered on November 13, 1862,*
> *Abraham Lincoln (1809–1865)*

"*Remember*," God said. But I had forgotten. Even though Nancy and the kids had continued to keep the Sabbath, I had allowed work to steal my day of rest. There is a subtle hubris to believing that work is so important that it requires our attention seven days a week.

Unlike ancient times, today very few of us are held slave against our will. Mostly, our slavery is self-imposed.

Mostly, we *forget* to be free.

Stop day has been reinstituted in our home. We guard it. It is something that all of us can do every week to help care for God's creation, both by what we decide *not to do*—buy things, answer e-mails, eat out—and by what we decide *to do*—take walks, read, and nap. By filling a well of peace, our family is able to resist the bombardment of messages screaming *buy, consume, bigger is better* the other six days of the week.

I pray that you, too, will find new ways to remember the Sabbath and reap the rewards of a weekly day of rest.

A world without a Sabbath would be like a man without a smile, like a summer without flowers, and like a homestead without a garden. It is the joyous day of the whole week.

In Ezra Taft Benson, Ensign,
Henry Ward Beecher (1813–1887)

Tending the Garden
What you can do to celebrate your day of rest

- Talk with your family about what a day of rest means and how you want to celebrate the Sabbath.
- Pick a cue (e-mail delivery chime, a glance at your watch) to remember Sabbath peace and look forward to your day of rest.
- Read Psalm 92, the psalm for the Sabbath day.
- Think ahead: clean the house and get errands done before the Sabbath begins.
- Take off your watch, and remove all reminders of work during the Sabbath day.
- Prepare a special Sabbath meal.
- Light Sabbath candles.
- Turn off your computer, and keep it off all day.
- Use the answering machine to screen calls.
- Bless your children and spouse on the Sabbath.
- Read Psalms 23, 24, 29, 93, 126, and 148 to remind yourself to care for God's creation throughout the week.
- Say grace before every meal on the Sabbath.
- Take a Sabbath walk.
- Spend at least ten minutes completely surrounded by nature each Sabbath.
- Spend at least half an hour in silence on the Sabbath.
- Fill a special box of books, art supplies, and toys for your children to be used only during quiet time on the Sabbath day.
- Ask for forgiveness.
- Invite someone to share a Sabbath meal.
- Read a book aloud.

- Take a daylong, family-wide criticism break.
- Avoid driving.
- Avoid eating out and buying things.

Adapted with permission from Go Green, Save Green: A Simple Guide to Saving Time, Money and God's Green Earth *(Nancy Sleeth, Tyndale, 2009). For more ideas, visit www.blessedearth.org.*

SIX

Gleaning
Ruth

Just then Boaz came from Bethlehem. He said to the reapers, "The Lord be with you." They answered, "The Lord bless you." Then Boaz said to his servant who was in charge of the reapers, "To whom does this young woman belong?" The servant who was in charge of the reapers answered, "She is the Moabite who came back with Naomi from the country of Moab. She said, 'Please, let me glean and gather among the sheaves behind the reapers.' So she came, and she has been on her feet from early this morning until now, without resting even for a moment."

Then Boaz said to Ruth, "Now listen, my daughter, do not go to glean in another field or leave this one, but keep close to my young women. Keep your eyes on the field that is being reaped, and follow behind them. I have ordered the young men not to bother you. If you get thirsty, go to the vessels and drink from what the young men have drawn." Then she fell prostrate, with her face to the ground, and said to him, "Why have I found favor in your sight, that you should take notice of me, when I am a foreigner?" But Boaz answered her, "All that you have done for your mother-in-law since the death of your husband has been fully told me, and how you left your father and mother and your native land and came to a people that you did not know before. May the Lord reward you for your deeds, and may you have a full reward from the Lord, the God of Israel,

under whose wings you have come for refuge!" Then she said,
"May I continue to find favor in your sight, my lord, for you
have comforted me and spoken kindly to your servant, even
though I am not one of your servants."

At mealtime Boaz said to her, "Come here, and eat some of
this bread, and dip your morsel in the sour wine." So she sat
beside the reapers, and he heaped up for her some parched
grain. She ate until she was satisfied, and she had some left
over. When she got up to glean, Boaz instructed his young men,
"Let her glean even among the standing sheaves, and do not
reproach her. You must also pull out some handfuls for her from
the bundles, and leave them for her to glean, and do not rebuke
her."

So she gleaned in the field until evening. Then she beat out
what she had gleaned, and it was about an ephah of barley. She
picked it up and came into the town, and her mother-in-law
saw how much she had gleaned. Then she took out and gave her
what was left over after she herself had been satisfied.

(Ruth 2:4–18)

Last fall, Nancy, our daughter, Emma, and I traveled to Nashville
to give a talk at a large youth-workers conference. We finished late
and looked for a place to grab a quick meal before calling it a night.
Our family tries not to eat at restaurants that serve on throwaway
plates—not always easy when we are on the road—but Emma spot-
ted a Panera up the hill, so we went there.

It was just before closing time. We each ordered a sandwich.
While the sandwiches were being prepared, we noticed that one of
the workers was unloading a whole glass case filled with brownies,
cookies, and slices of chocolate-lovers cake and placing the desserts

> *"I give you a new commandment, that you love one another. Just as I
> have loved you, you also should love one another" (John 13:34).*

in large plastic containers. Next he emptied eight bagel bins into large trash bags. Then came the loaves of fresh bread—there were at least twenty of them, baked with an array of grains and fillings—enough to fill another large trash bag. A pregnant woman at the table behind us worked efficiently, dumping all the coffee into a five-gallon bucket and cream into a thermos. When I asked where all this food was headed, she replied, "To the homeless shelter." The items were collected and out the door before we finished our sandwiches. Not a crumb of Panera's breads were wasted. They went to the orphans, the widows, and the least among us. The bakery's leftovers were gleaned for the homeless Ruths and Naomis of Nashville.

Could Panera have maximized profits by selling leftovers at 50 percent off during the last hour of business, or selling them as "manager's specials" the following day? Yes, but they chose not to. Instead, they honored the millennia-old principles of gleaning.

Today the vast majority of us are not farmers. Yet the principles of gleaning and care for the poor are as timeless as the book of Ruth. Panera is one example of a modern-day Boaz, the farmer who allowed the widow Ruth to glean in his fields. But who are the modern-day Ruths and Naomis?

The twenty-first-century Ruth that I will use as an illustration is new in town. She is from East Africa, and through an improbable and unfortunate series of events, she finds herself a refugee in the Northeast Kingdom of Vermont. Young, widowed, and homeless, she has no green card. For half the year this remote corner of northern New England is snow covered. Her husband, an American, grew up in this place where trees turn bright yellow and orange in fall and give maple syrup when the days turn warm at winter's end. When Ruth and her husband lived together under the equatorial sun, she

> "Beloved, let us love one another, because love is from God; everyone who loves is born of God and knows God. Whoever does not love does not know God, for God is love" (1 John 4:7–8).

hadn't fully appreciated the foreignness of his American world. He so effortlessly fit into Africa. They met when he was finishing his residency at Tenwick Hospital. They married despite the differences in their skin colors and being raised on two different continents. "Our children will have hybrid vigor," he would joke.

He'd trained for general surgery. That was his mission and his calling: heal the sick. Once, when his mother questioned why he wouldn't practice in the States, he'd explained, "If you saw ten people carrying a heavy log, and nine of the people were lifting one end, and only one was at the other end—which end would it make sense to help carry?" So he married Ruth and the medical needs of eastern Africa.

In the end his death seemed so stupid, so pointless—he'd gotten sick from bad water. In less than two days his vascular system collapsed. It was probably cholera, although no one was certain.

Ruth had used her meager savings to fly to the States and spread her husband's ashes on a Vermont hillside. It was the least that Ruth could do for her mother-in-law, Naomi. It was what Naomi had wanted.

The son had gone away a vigorous, laughing man and come back as a tin full of ash. Naomi caught a chill, and suffered a stroke two days after the ceremony. She was moved from her retirement apartment to the hospital, with the unfortunate result that Ruth could not live with her—as was their original plan. If Ruth had known the system, if the apartment manager hadn't cared about crossing the t's and dotting the i's . . . but the end result was that the manager had put Ruth out on the street.

On this afternoon, Ruth perches on the edge of a heavy armchair in the town library scanning the Help Wanted section of the local newspaper. The paper is held by its spine in a walnut holder that matches the library's Victorian tables, bookcases, and newspaper

"Do to others as you would have them do to you" (Luke 6:31).

racks. One of the paper's ads promises "a thousand dollars a week—for motivated self-starters." Ruth reads on, looking for something like "hard work at a minimum wage—no green card required," but to no avail. Ruth slowly and carefully replaces the newspaper in the rack. She glances at the magazines on display. The cover of *People* says "Stars Drop 20 Pounds in 20 Days." Ruth's stomach growls. She is homeless and hungry in a land of second homes and obesity. What Ruth would like is rice and beans.

Ruth walks down High Street, past several shops that have gone out of business. She glances in the window of one clothing shop, A Woman of Substance, the store "for the woman with more. Sizes 20 and up." In four more hours Ruth can return to the shelter.

There is a McDonald's at the corner of Veterans Bridge. It is a good place to use the washroom and sit for a moment. A man in a camouflage jacket and bright orange hat abandons an uneaten portion of a triple-layered burger. He walks out leaving the tray on the table. Just as Ruth moves toward the abandoned meal, an employee descends, wads the paper and food into a tight ball, and shoves it deep into the waste bin.

Outside it is cold. The afternoon's grey sky matches the road salt and melting slush on the streets. Three hours and change until the shelter opens.

The town has two main groceries. The larger one is part of a big chain, and the other is a small independent store. Large chains universally lock up the food being thrown out, but the small one has a regular Dumpster crowned by two large lids made of plastic. On the sides of the Dumpster are two-and-a-half-foot doors that slide to allow access to the steel container's contents.

Ruth approaches as inconspicuously as is possible for a homeless African woman on foot in an all-white town of auto travel. Good—no

> *"Those who oppress the poor insult their Maker, but those who are kind to the needy honor him"* (Prov. 14:31).

one seems to notice as she slides open the Dumpster's side door. Under
a pile of cardboard she sees a wrapped deli sandwich, and a package of
chicken thighs encased in pale yellow Styrofoam and clear cellophane.
She pushes aside the cardboard and trash.

"Hey! You! What are you doing?"

The man shouting from the loading dock has his head covered by
a blue hairnet. He exhales from his just-lit cigarette. "You're not supposed to be in there. This is private property."

> "The king will say to those at his right hand, 'Come, you that are
> blessed by my Father, inherit the kingdom prepared for you from the
> foundation of the world; for I was hungry and you gave me food, I
> was thirsty and you gave me something to drink, I was a stranger and
> you welcomed me, I was naked and you gave me clothing, I was sick
> and you took care of me, I was in prison and you visited me.'
>
> "Then the righteous will answer him, 'Lord, when was it that we saw
> you hungry and gave you food, or thirsty and gave you something
> to drink? And when was it that we saw you a stranger and welcomed
> you, or naked and gave you clothing? And when was it that we saw
> you sick or in prison and visited you?' And the king will answer them,
> 'Truly I tell you, just as you did it to one of the least of these who are
> members of my family, you did it to me.'
>
> "Then he will say to those at his left hand, 'You that are accursed,
> depart from me into the eternal fire prepared for the devil and his
> angels; for I was hungry and you gave me no food, I was thirsty
> and you gave me nothing to drink, I was a stranger and you did not
> welcome me, naked and you did not give me clothing, sick and in
> prison and you did not visit me.'
>
> "Then they also will answer, 'Lord, when was it that we saw you
> hungry or thirsty or a stranger or naked or sick or in prison, and did
> not take care of you?' Then he will answer them, 'Truly I tell you, just
> as you did not do it to one of the least of these, you did not do it to
> me'" (Matt. 25:34–45).

"I'm sorry," Ruth mumbles. Shame constricts her throat as she backs away from her accuser.

The man takes a drag from his cigarette and aims it at Ruth's face. "Put back what you've stolen." Ruth glances down at the day-old sandwich in her hand, then tosses the meal back into the green Dumpster and begins walking toward the shelter.

Our modern-day Ruth—homeless in Vermont—is analogous to the Bible's Ruth. The book of Ruth is a four-page vignette found between the books of Judges and 1 Samuel in the Old Testament. The original Ruth found herself widowed and homeless in the country of Moab, which is Israel's neighbor to the east. She threw her lot in with her mother-in-law, Naomi, and also with Naomi's God, who happens to be the God of Abraham, Isaac, and Jacob.

> Ruth replied, "Don't urge me to leave you or to turn back from you. Where you go I will go, and where you stay I will stay. Your people will be my people and your God my God.
>
> Where you die I will die, and there I will be buried. May the LORD deal with me, be it ever so severely, if anything but death separates you and me." *(Ruth 1:16–17, NIV)*

This beautiful declaration of loyalty is made by Ruth to her mother-in-law as the two women journey back to Bethlehem, the place of Naomi's birth. In the grand scheme of the Bible's story of redemption, the two are moving toward the Messiah, who will be born

---

"Let each of you look not to your own interests, but to the interests of others. Let the same mind be in you that was in Christ Jesus, who, though he was in the form of God, did not regard equality with God as something to be exploited, but emptied himself, taking the form of a slave, being born in human likeness. And being found in human form, he humbled himself and became obedient to the point of death—even death on a cross" (Phil. 2:4–8).

in Bethlehem. Ruth will rock the cradles of David, Solomon, and the baby Jesus. Indeed, Ruth, not from a Jewish background, is even listed in Christ's genealogy (Matt. 1:5). Tracing lineage through the paternal—not the maternal—side is the accepted way that the Hebrews tracked family trees. Something extraordinary is signified by the inclusion of Ruth in Christ's family tree.

One of the most touching aspects of Ruth's story is steadfast love, shown through the practice of gleaning food for her mother-in-law. In order to understand how far we have diverged from the biblical mandates concerning land, crops, and animals, consider the following scenario:

You are a farmer. You have a field of corn that is ripe. A man comes down the road. He is hungry. He picks an ear of corn and eats it. Has he committed a crime?

I asked this hypothetical question at a college recently, and the consensus was that the man in question is stealing—and thus committing a crime: "Thou shalt not steal."

But what does the Bible have to say about gleaning?

If you go into your neighbor's vineyard, you may eat your fill of grapes, as many as you wish, but you shall not put any in a container. If you go into your neighbor's standing grain, you may pluck the ears with your hand, but you shall not put a sickle to your neighbor's standing grain. *(Deut. 23:24–25)*

"Hear what the Lord says: Rise, plead your case before the mountains, and let the hills hear your voice. Hear, you mountains, the controversy of the Lord, and you enduring foundations of the earth; for the Lord has a controversy with his people, and he will contend with Israel. 'O my people, what have I done to you? In what have I wearied you? Answer me! For I brought you up from the land of Egypt, and redeemed you from the house of slavery; and I sent before you Moses, Aaron, and Miriam'" (Mic. 6:1–4).

Quoting Deuteronomy is, of course, citing Old Testament theology. To learn what the New Testament has to say, we can look at the very actions of Christ.

At that time Jesus went through the grainfields on the sabbath; his disciples were hungry, and they began to pluck heads of grain to eat. When the Pharisees saw it, they said to him, "Look, your disciples are doing what is not lawful to do on the sabbath." *(Matt. 12:1–2)*

Jesus and his followers are not accused of breaking the law because they are stealing grain—but because they are working on the Sabbath. They have a right to the grain.

In the book of Ruth, the protagonist gleans in a field belonging to her mother-in-law's relative Boaz. Like our African woman in Vermont (without a green card), Ruth is in society's most precarious position. But Boaz welcomes Ruth to the field. He orders his harvesters to get sloppy when they bundle the barley. This injunction allows the widow Ruth to obtain more food because more barley is lying on the ground.

Likewise, the Bible instructs the owners of orchards and vineyards to leave behind grapes and grain that have been dropped. They are not to harvest to the very ends of the field—but to let a certain portion of crop stand unpicked, thus allowing food to be available for the widow, orphan, immigrant, and the wild animals (Deut. 24:19; Lev. 19:9–10).

> "'Will the LORD be pleased with thousands of rams, with ten thousands of rivers of oil? Shall I give my firstborn for my transgression, the fruit of my body for the sin of my soul?' He has told you, O mortal, what is good; and what does the LORD require of you but to do justice, and to love kindness, and to walk humbly with your God?" (Mic. 6:7–8).

Owners of olive trees are instructed not to beat the boughs of the trees twice, but to provide for the needs of the poor and wildlife by leaving fruit on the trees. Olive oil was one of Israel's most valuable cash crops. The oil is dense in calories and easily stored—no refrigeration needed. It was a key export and, like wine or honey, could be "banked" for a rainy day. Yet what is at work in these biblical principles is not maximized profits for owners or shareholders, but long-term prosperity for all.

Where does this come into play in our modern lives?

We certainly have food aplenty in our society and much food waste. Estimates vary, but somewhere between 30 and 50 percent of the food in this country is simply thrown away. According to the University of Arizona's Garbage Project, every American tosses 1.3 pounds of food per day.

I got interested in the amount of food thrown away at the retail level after watching the documentary *The Gleaners and I*. Like my modern-day Ruth, I gleaned from grocery store Dumpsters for several weeks. Nancy had a Mother's Day dinner entirely out of the trash. We served cherry pies from crates of fruit that had been tossed.

To set your minds at ease, I did this experiment in cool weather. The entire world acted as a refrigeration unit. My subsequent conversations with store workers have revealed a prevalent attitude of hostility toward Dumpster divers/gleaners. The exceptions occur when owners and managers show leadership in the area of charity.

Often the feelings we have about the food or other things we cast off is that it is trash. But one man's trash is another's meal. At a Christian music concert, we collected recyclable bottles out of

> "Thus says the LORD: Act with justice and righteousness, and deliver from the hand of the oppressor anyone who has been robbed. And do no wrong or violence to the alien, the orphan, and the widow, or shed innocent blood in this place" (Jer. 22:3).

the trash. It was blistering hot, yet we found many unopened water bottles in the Dumpsters, as well as enough personal pizzas in unopened boxes to feed the town's homeless population for a week.

And we don't only throw away perfectly good food. There is no end to what we throw in the waste bin daily: cell phones, televisions, and ships are among the many thousand of things society manufactures, uses for a while, and discards. But there is a problem with throwing away. There is no "away." There is no magical place where old products disappear once they are no longer wanted.

Recycling is one way we can deal more responsibly with disposal; however, it is an imperfect solution. Many of us have seen documentaries detailing the hazards of ship breaking in Bangladesh. Huge vessels are torn apart, and in the process oil leaks out into the Indian Ocean. Workers toil in substandard conditions. And it is not just old cargo ships that have toxic residues when dismantled. Most modern products also have toxic elements and are not made with disposal in mind.

One approach has been to ban the export of things such as retired ships. But what of those whose lives depend on disassembling old telephones and ships, or eating discarded food? The simple biblical answer is that they have a right to the things we cast off. Nowhere is this more evident than in Jesus' parable of the rich man and Lazarus.

There was a rich man who was dressed in purple and fine linen and who feasted sumptuously every day.

And at his gate lay a poor man named Lazarus, covered with sores, who longed to satisfy his hunger with what fell from

> *"Give the king your justice, O God, and your righteousness to a king's son. . . . For he delivers the needy when they call, the poor and those who have no helper. He has pity on the weak and the needy, and saves the lives of the needy. From oppression and violence he redeems their life; and precious is their blood in his sight" (Ps. 72:1, 12–14).*

the rich man's table; even the dogs would come and lick his sores. The poor man died and was carried away by the angels to be with Abraham. The rich man also died and was buried. In Hades, where he was being tormented, he looked up and saw Abraham far away with Lazarus by his side.

He called out, "Father Abraham, have mercy on me, and send Lazarus to dip the tip of his finger in water and cool my tongue; for I am in agony in these flames."

But Abraham said, "Child, remember that during your lifetime you received your good things, and Lazarus in like manner evil things; but now he is comforted here, and you are in agony. Besides all this, between you and us a great chasm has been fixed, so that those who might want to pass from here to you cannot do so, and no one can cross from there to us." (Luke 16:19–26)

As with many of Jesus' parables, the story has multiple levels of meaning. On one level it is a story of poverty and charity—or rather the lack of charity. Lazarus wants only the scraps from the wealthy. What we consider as trash is a valuable resource for others.

Do we believe that we own everything in our yards, our houses, our garages? If we live according to the biblical principles that allowed Jesus and his disciples to glean grain, the answer is no. Part of everything we "own" belongs to "Ruth." To adhere to that principle in a nonagrarian society might mean your next cell phone or computer purchase takes into account how toxic it is to recycle. It might

"[Jesus] said to him, 'You shall love the Lord your God with all your heart, and with all your soul, and with all your mind.' This is the greatest and first commandment. And a second is like it: 'You shall love your neighbor as yourself.' On these two commandments hang all the law and the prophets" (Matt. 22:37–40).

mean supporting restaurants, grocers, and bakeries that have programs to distribute leftover food at the end of the day.

How can you know which businesses to support? Talk to local restaurant owners about how they dispose of their leftovers. Same goes for the cafeteria at work or school, and even your church. If you own a home, start a garden and share the produce. Or organize a community garden and provide fresh produce to a homeless shelter.

Then do some research at www.betterworldshopper.org. Companies like Ben & Jerry's, Stonyfield Farm, Bob's Red Mill, Eden Foods, King Arthur, Annie's, Cascadian Farm, Seeds of Change, and Newman's Own as well as various grocery stores have longstanding reputations for being the Boazes of the food business. Look for businesses that give leftovers to the poor, and then support them.

We may not always have a way to pass along extra food or castoff products to the poor, but we can decide where and how we spend our money. For many of us, this is the most significant way we can become modern-day Boazes and help the Ruths and Naomis of our world.

One of the greatest injustices in the contemporary world consists precisely in this: that the ones who possess much are relatively few and those who possess almost nothing are many. It is the injustice of the poor distribution of the goods and services originally intended for all.

Papal Encyclical "Sollicitudo Rei Socialis," Vatican City, 1988, #26–28, Pope John Paul II (1920–2005)

Tending the Garden
What you can do to share with the poor

- Start a garden and share the produce with others.

- Organize a church or community garden, and provide fresh, organic produce to a nearby homeless shelter.

- Organize an urban garden, so people who live in apartments can grow their own food.

- Collect leftovers from church functions—weddings, luncheons, coffee hour—and give to the homeless.

- Ask local grocers and restaurant owners what they do with leftovers at the end of the day. Volunteer to start a second-harvest collection system.

- Research environmentally and socially responsible companies at www.betterworldshopper.org, and then support those businesses, even if it costs a little more.

- Fast one meal per week, or forgo carry-out coffee in the morning, then donate that saved money to a soup kitchen.

- Give up one food item for Lent, and then donate that money.

- Use a skill, or develop one. Refurbish unwanted computers, bicycles, furniture, etc., and donate it to refugees who come with nothing.

- Volunteer at a soup kitchen, homeless shelter, or refugee ministry.

- Organize a furniture drive for a ministry.

- Contact your local homeless shelter, food pantry, and refugee ministry. Ask them to keep you posted on urgent needs. Then send out e-mails to friends, and offer your home or church as a drop-off point.

- Weigh how much food your family wastes in one week. Then set a goal of reducing that waste by at least 10 percent this year.

- If you are connected with a school, suggest that the cafeteria go trayless. Students will waste (literally) tons less food.

- Clean out your closets, garage, and basement. List unneeded items on www.freecycle.org, or donate to Goodwill, Salvation Army, or a ministry.

- Donate children's books and toys to a day-care center or after-school program.

- Set up a free table at church, or a bulletin board that posts items that you no longer need. Free exchanges can also be listed on the Web.

- Donate or loan your second car to a refugee family, or a family that lost a job and can no longer afford car payments.

Adapted with permission from Go Green, Save Green: A Simple Guide to Saving Time, Money and God's Green Earth *(Nancy Sleeth, Tyndale, 2009). For more ideas, visit www.blessedearth.org*

SEVEN

God the Creator
Job

Have you comprehended the expanse of the earth? Declare, if
you know all this. Where is the way to the dwelling of light,
and where is the place of darkness, that you may take it to
its territory and that you may discern the paths to its home?
Surely you know, for you were born then, and the number of
your days is great! Have you entered the storehouses of the
snow, or have you seen the storehouses of the hail, which I
have reserved for the time of trouble, for the day of battle and
war? What is the way to the place where the light is distributed,
or where the east wind is scattered upon the earth?
Who has cut a channel for the torrents of rain, and a way for
the thunderbolt, to bring rain on a land where no one lives, on
the desert, which is empty of human life, to satisfy the waste
and desolate land, and to make the ground put forth grass? Has
the rain a father, or who has begotten the drops of dew? From
whose womb did the ice come forth, and who has given birth
to the hoarfrost of heaven? The waters become hard like stone,
and the face of the deep is frozen. Can you bind the chains of
the Pleiades, or loose the cords of Orion? Can you lead forth
the Mazzaroth in their season, or can you guide the Bear with
its children? Do you know the ordinances of the heavens? Can
you establish their rule on the earth? Can you lift up your
voice to the clouds, so that a flood of waters may cover you?

Can you send forth lightnings, so that they may go and say to you, "Here we are"? Who has put wisdom in the inward parts, or given understanding to the mind? Who has the wisdom to number the clouds? Or who can tilt the waterskins of the heavens, when the dust runs into a mass and the clods cling together? *(Job 38:18–38)*

Lester K. Slate woke when the alarm told him to—at 6:36 a.m. It was a Friday in October 1979. The alarm didn't beep or clang but made a small, pleasant sound like the high C on an elementary-school xylophone. The clock was a six-month-old wedding gift from the sister of his wife, Melody, who lived in California. She'd said something about its balancing the day, and how they should wake slowly and remember their dreams. Lester's sister-in-law had also given them a journal to record their spiritual journeys—but Melody had started pasting recipes into the dream book instead.

"I married the right sister," Lester mused as he pushed the silence button on the alarm. "Not the fruitcake." Setting the time for 6:36 instead of 6:30 was Lester's idea, the symmetry appealing to the machinist part of his brain. He always enjoyed glancing over at a clock that read 11:11 or 2:02. Besides, it gave him six more minutes in bed with his new wife.

By 7:07 Lester was headed north across the bridge in his Ford F-150 pickup. He stopped and paid the toll, then exited at the first off ramp. At the drive-in at Mickey D's, he handed money to the cashier at the first window and then picked up his coffee and the bag containing three sausage biscuits at the second window.

"Have a great day!" the woman called through the speaker.

> **God created the earth. It all belongs to him.**
>
> "The earth is the LORD's and all that is in it, the world, and those who live in it" (Ps. 24:1).

"Got to—it's Friday," Lester returned. He put the truck in drive and started on the last of his commute—3.6 miles, more or less—along the bay front up to the airport industrial park. He parked at GTI Industries, grabbed his lunch pail, and headed toward the building.

"Hey, Les, what's happening?" Chuck held the entrance door open for his friend.

"Thank God it's Friday," Lester half-spoke, half-sang. They threw their lunches into their lockers, then lined up to start the shift.

"Yeah, like you've got any worries any day of the week—new Master's union card, new truck, new wife, new house. What you need is a few snotty-nosed kids screaming and climbing the curtains like the rest of us. Speaking of which—you and the missus wouldn't want to come watch our kids this evening, would you?"

"Thanks, but no thanks, Chuckie."

They both reached the head of the line and punched in.

GTI manufactured almost-one-of-a-kind stainless-steel fabrications for the navy. Lester spent the morning milling a gimbal used on the decks of AEGIS-class destroyers.

At lunchtime, the buzzer blew, and then an announcement came over the horn directing all employees to the loading bay.

"What's this about, Les?"

"No clue, Chuck; could be another one of those random navy shakedowns looking for nuclear missiles in our lockers."

But that's not what it turned out to be. The factory was shutting down. Everybody got the pink slip. They had fifteen minutes to clear out and then line up to have anything they were taking home searched. There was no real explanation.

God loves all of his creation.

"He determines the number of the stars; he gives to all of them their names. Great is our LORD, and abundant in power; his understanding is beyond measure" (Ps. 147:4–5).

"Tough break, guys," the super said. "You know those cuts made in the defense budget last year? This here's the trickle down."

"Welcome to the union," one of the older guys said.

Lester started his engine and headed toward home. *What about the payments on the truck? And the house?* He'd never been laid off or fired before. An underlying sense of shame began welling up, even though getting booted had nothing to do with his work performance. Still, he needed to tell Melody. Today was her day off. *She had been talking about starting a family. But now they didn't have any health insurance.*

His friend Chuck was right. He and Melody had everything going for them. The worst-case scenario was that he wouldn't be able to get another job within commuting distance and they'd have to move. *That was it—the worst.* They might have to wait on the family thing, too—but that was okay with Lester; it could be the silver lining in the whole thing, as his dad would say.

Lester pulled into their street, an old-fashioned neighborhood with front porches and a crazy blind left turn. They were the "third house on the left after the sharp left."

Parked behind Melody's copper colored Maverick was his best friend, Tim's, unmistakable orange Camaro with twin white racing stripes. He pulled into the driveway, got out, and stared at the two cars.

Melody came out the front door and closed it behind her. She looked at him, and he knew that nothing good was going to happen—yet it was going to happen anyway.

"Oh, Les, we've got to talk."

The earth that God created is endlessly varied and interconnected.

"O Lord, how manifold are your works! In wisdom you have made them all; the earth is full of your creatures" (Ps. 104:24).

"Melody! I just got laid off, and you're home getting . . ."

Lester ran back to the truck, and Melody called, "Lester! Les! I didn't mean to . . ."

Her plea was drowned by the engine roar as Lester did a three-point turn, running onto the lawn. There was a split second when he thought of backing around too fast and hitting Tim's car, but he didn't.

He'd lost his job, his wife, his house, and his best friend. So he drove to his older brother's house and spent the night. On Saturday morning, his brother decided to take Lester out hunting—to cheer him up. They had grown up hunting together, and it was certain to get Lester's mind off things.

That was when I met Lester—just after his big brother accidentally shot him. Lester was brought to the emergency department with shotgun wounds to the face, shoulder, and right forearm. They were not fatal, nor even deforming.

I always think of Lester when I am having a bad day and wonder how his life got on. The problem with being an ER doctor is living with the mystery of not knowing. If I tell the story of Lester out loud, it gets a laugh. There is still hope left at the end. Lester is young. But there are stories from the ER without hope or humor. The good guys don't make it, the lump in the young mother's breast doesn't go away at the end of the pregnancy, and we are left wondering about why there is so much suffering in the world.

The book of Job is all about the problem of suffering, and bad things happening to good people. Job wasn't just a nice guy who

---

God's creation is intended to sustain us. We are to use it, not abuse it.

"You visit the earth and water it, you greatly enrich it; the river of God is full of water; you provide the people with grain, for so you have prepared it" (Ps. 65:9).

paid his taxes on time and put 10 percent in the plate on Sundays. Job is described as being "blameless and upright, one who feared God and turned away from evil." He never looked at another's wife with lust or failed to help a widow, orphan, or poor person. He never lied. NEVER. In other words, he wasn't like you or me. He was blameless, which makes him better than Adam and Eve. In fact he is almost unique in the Bible. He is a prototype of one who lives like Christ.

Job has it all, and then one day he loses it all. First, the cattle are stolen and the farmhands are killed. Then all the sheep and shepherds are toasted. Then the Chaldeans steal the camels and kill the camel drivers. Lastly, all his children are killed when the family house falls down.

Still, Job says, "Praise the Lord."

His wife advises, "Curse God and die."

Next Job loses his health. Covered in boils, he sits on a dung heap outside the city. He scrapes away at the oozing pustules with a potsherd, and is joined by three friends and one young onlooker.

Over the millennia there has been endless commentary on the back and forth between Job, Eliphaz, Bildad, Zophar, and Elihu. What could we add to it? Their conversation sounds like that of a husband and wife stuck in a never-ending fight. Each side keeps saying the same thing—just louder. What interests me is what God (Elihu) has to say. God's soliloquy begins in chapter 38 and runs until chapter 42. These five chapters are without question the longest communication from God within the Bible—from his lips to our ears. God has a whole lot more to say here than "*I AM WHO I AM*" (Exod. 3:14).

God wants creation to be celebrated.

"Let the heavens be glad, and let the earth rejoice; let the sea roar, and all that fills it; let the field exult, and everything in it. Then shall all the trees of the forest sing for joy" (Ps. 96:11–12).

What does God talk about in his longest speech in the Bible? God does not directly answer why bad things happen to good people or why Job is afflicted with bad luck when he is blameless. The longest speech by God is really about his creation. "Where were you, Job, when I started this whole thing? Where were you when I laid the foundations of the earth?"

God's response to Job and his friends is *Be humble*. He goes on to describe the beginning when all *"the morning stars sang together."* God the Creator *"made the clouds its garment, and thick darkness its swaddling band."* God *"prescribed bounds for it, and set bars and doors, and said, 'Thus far shall you come, and no farther, and here shall your proud waves be stopped'"* (Job 38:7–11). By describing creation, God is chastising Job and his friends: it is hubris to think that people can know more than God. He set up the world. He put it in motion. And he sustains it all.

God's advice: *"Be still, and know that I am God"* (Ps. 46:10).

Over the last several years, I've been given many Bibles with commentaries. Some of the graphs, charts, and notations have been quite helpful in learning to understand the Scriptures, but much of the commentary revolves around a sort of what-does-this-all-mean-to-me approach—or some variation on the personal, twenty-first-century iGod.

What's curious is that these commentaries have remarkably little to say about God's speech to Job. It's as if the longest speech by God doesn't really count for much. If it did, perhaps we'd have to pay more attention to the stars, birds, and endangered species—because that is what God draws our attention to. If we gave much thought to the

---

God wants us to learn from creation.

"The heavens are telling the glory of God; and the firmament proclaims his handiwork. Day to day pours forth speech, and night to night declares knowledge" (Ps. 19:1–2).

Creator's longest speech, we'd have to live more meek and humble lives.

Technology has only increased our hubris. Job and his friends had not walked on the surface of the sea, nor had they comprehended the expanse of the earth. But we moderns have. Job and his friends were humbled by God's speech, but we are not. Yet we should be—perhaps more than any previous generation. Because technology allows us to do more harm, more quickly, to more of God's creation, God's message is more relevant than ever. We don't need more wonders, but rather a greater sense of wonderment. Just look: it's all around us. This message, despite all our scientific advances, is timeless. We do not need to dash off to the South Pole or fly to the Galapagos Islands to see God's majesty. His creation can be found right off the back porch at the bird feeder. What we need is a change of heart—and a change of perspective.

We need to become nature lovers—because God is one. Does God concern himself with an endangered species of desert grass being bulldozed into extinction? Most definitely, if you believe what the Bible says:

Who has cut a channel for the torrents of rain
and a way for the thunderbolt,
to bring rain on a land where no one lives,
on the desert, which is empty of human life,
to satisfy the waste and desolate land,
and to make the ground put forth grass? *(Job 38:25–27)*

One lesson we can gain from God's creation is a humble attitude.

"Ask the animals, and they will teach you; the birds of the air, and they will tell you; ask the plants of the earth, and they will teach you; and the fish of the sea will declare to you. Who among all these does not know that the hand of the LORD has done this? In his hand is the life of every living thing and the breath of every human being" (Job 12:7–10).

This Scripture passage makes explicit that God is the agent who sends rain to the wilderness, and that the grass in those desolate places has meaning beyond what Job and his friends can reason or assign. Wilderness matters.

What God is saying is that humanity is not the be-all and end-all of the entire universe. We are not the center of everything. The more subtle message might even be that misery and suffering will follow if we believe too much in our self-importance.

I am not formally trained as a theologian, and yet I am often invited to seminaries to talk about this area of theology that has been largely abandoned for the last century: God the Creator who reveals himself through his creation. I am humbled by the depth of knowledge and inquiry at these institutions, yet there is a related area in which (looking on as an outsider) I believe the teaching is almost universally off track.

I think that we need to pay more attention to the peculiar language of Jesus. Even a casual reader of the Gospels can see that Christ's language is particularly organic, or earthy. This should not be surprising, if we have looked carefully at the words of his Father in the book of Job. In Job, God the Father uses organic language (relating to living, carbon-based things) to answer humanity's questions. In the Gospels, Jesus the Son constantly draws upon organic metaphors in his discussion of the world's redemption. The language of the Father is reflected in the language of the Son. Both draw attention to nature as a path to knowledge—a way to learn about the Artist from his art.

Our hearts grow more grateful when we praise God's creation.

"Praise him, sun and moon; praise him, all you shining stars! Praise him, you highest heavens, and you waters above the heavens! Let them praise the name of the Lord, for he commanded and they were created. He established them forever and ever; he fixed their bounds, which cannot be passed" (Ps. 148:3–6).

Again and again in the Gospels, we see Christ reiterating and underlining the wonderment of God the Creator. *God*, he says, *is the kind of God who groans when a single sparrow falls from the sky. He is the sort of God that clothes every flower, and lily of the field.* Until we can comprehend how much God loves a flower, we will never comprehend how much he cares about each and every one of us.

Jesus continues his Father's organic language throughout the parables. For example, when asked what the kingdom of heaven is like, Jesus replies that it is like *"someone who sowed good seed"* (Matt. 13:24); or *"if someone would scatter seed on the ground"* (Mark 4:26); or *"a mustard seed that someone took and sowed in his field"* (Matt. 13:31). In fact, Jesus' language gets so full of yeast, vines, and soil that it makes me want to put on my overalls and gardening gloves. Jesus didn't just retreat to the wilderness; he taught on mountains, in fields, and beside the sea.

Now the standard knee-jerk reaction is that "Jesus is just speaking in the vernacular." This response boils down to one of two things: either Jesus is a country bumpkin, or he has condescended to speak in the everyday language of the people. I don't believe either is the case. Think about the vernacular of a preacher today. During the playoffs, a minister might talk about "playing a winning game for Jesus." Sports were just as big a deal in the Roman world of Jesus' era as they are today (think Colosseum), yet they are completely absent from his vocabulary. And preachers today don't talk about the humdrum world of work either. We hear few

> **Most important, we can learn about the character of the Creator through his creation.**
>
> *"Ever since the creation of the world his eternal power and divine nature, invisible though they are, have been understood and seen through the things he has made. So they are without excuse"* (Rom. 1:20).

"relevant" sermons today that focus on staffing charts, copying machines, or the coffeemaker.

Another bit of evidence about Christ's language choices is that these organic analogies are virtually absent from the writings of Paul, not to mention the letters of the other apostles. Further, there are no contemporaries of Christ who communicate in the same manner: Cicero, Livius, and the Talmudic rabbis are not discussing four soil types. Lastly, Jesus' own disciples don't even understand his language. The parable of the four soils must be explained to them.

Isn't it fitting that the God who answers Job out of the whirl-wind—who points to stars, lightning, snow, lions, wild ox, and the hippopotamus to explain the workings of the universe—would send a Son that spoke the same way?

Jesus is an outdoorsy guy because God made the outdoors. We have a contemporary church saying that is so overused it has almost lost its meaning—yet it gets at one of the great foibles of humanity. It concerns Job and his friends and how we attempt to make God as small as ourselves. We are forever endeavoring to "put God in a box." Nothing can be truer of our generation than the phenomenon of our trying to keep God indoors—in an air-conditioned building where the windows are sealed shut.

By downplaying his organic language, we put Christ in a cubicle instead of recognizing that his communication is capable of reaching across generations and technologies. Christ walks on the water, takes money from the mouth of a fish, and rides an unbroken colt. He is master of the created world because his Father has put him in

---

Just as God uses creation to teach, Jesus, the incarnate God, uses organic language to share the gospel.

"I am the true vine, and my Father is the vinegrower. . . . Those who abide in me and I in them bear much fruit" (John 15:1, 5).

charge of all things. To take away the importance of nature is to diminish his kingdom on earth.

Children of the current generation spend about 1 percent of their lives out of doors, and nearly 30 percent in front of a screen. Parents and grandparents must get/let the kids outdoors. This is not a matter of where you live—every place has some outside. It is a matter of making it happen, and making it a priority.

Across the street from me lives a nine-year-old boy. I am fascinated with Earl because, unlike many of the other kids in our town, he does not live indoors. When I walk up the street, there's Earl running behind a bush with a stick in his hand. He plays out imaginary battles with dozens of enemies every day. His life is rich because he knows every tree and bush in the neighborhood.

When I was in medical school, we lived in a large city, yet I had more access to trees and streams than I do today, living in a small college town. The city fathers and mothers of a generation ago understood the importance of parks and outdoor recreation. Still, we must look for nature where we live rather than dashing all about the planet loving it to death. You can meditate on a single plant and find a world there.

This past spring, I noticed my next door neighbor Hank admiring the leaves of the fruit trees we'd planted last year. I walked out one morning and asked what he saw. He gave me a leaf-by-leaf tour of the young trees, including how the ants herded aphids onto a few select leaves. The ants protect the tree in this manner and then

---

Jesus does some of his most important teaching on mountains and beside rivers. He teaches on field trips.

"When Jesus saw the crowds, he went up the mountain; and after he sat down, his disciples came to him. Then he began to speak, and taught them" (Matt. 5:1–2).

know where to find the aphids to snack on later. Hank saw an entire world on a new pear tree; his remarks bring to mind the poet Blake's observation: "To see the world in a grain of sand, and heaven in a wild flower/Hold infinity in the palm of your hand, and eternity in an hour."

Certain activities naturally seem to go together and build synergistically upon one another. One such combination is Sabbath and a walk in the woods. God sends the simple and the unexpected at these moments. One finds a cardinal in the snowbound thicket, or deer among the laurel.

Since childhood, I have been fond of days that are on the brisk side. I can occasionally find complete and supreme contentment lying on a south-facing bank, looking skyward, and basking in the sun's rays. It is one thing to read or recite the Twenty-third Psalm, but it is a quantum more to actually live it.

When is the last time you held a turtle or a toad? They will not often hop out from under the living-room couch. They must be sought in the outdoors. When was the last time you took your child or grandchild and walked to a stream, then simply stopped and looked at the water flow? When was the last time you tried to make sense out of the shapes in cumulus clouds?

The wonder of God's speech to Job is that we cannot figure out or solve everything. We are not meant to. But we can marvel along with the God of all creation—at the creation. All we need are open minds and an appreciation that we are part of something bigger than ourselves.

If we want to learn more about God, all we have to do is step outside and read "the other book," written in nature.

The initial step for a soul to come to knowledge of God is contemplation of nature.

Irenaeus (c. 120–c. 202)

Wonder at a leaf, icicle, sparrow, or cloud of stars. Notice in what quadrant the constellations rise and set. Sing with the morning stars.

The next time you find yourself losing your job, your best friend, your health—like the Old Testament figure Job, or my unfortunate patient Lester—look for consolation in God's creation. Be humble. Be still. Lie down in green pastures and sit beside quiet waters, and you will behold the face of God.

We cannot love what we do not know. Get to know God's creation, and you will become a friend of God.

Reading about nature is fine, but if a person walks in the woods and listens carefully, he can learn more than what is in books, for they speak with the voice of God.

George Washington Carver (1864–1943)

Tending the Garden
What you can do to celebrate creation

- Spend at least five minutes quietly in nature each day: "Be still, and know that I am God."
- Check the weather forecast and schedule a good night for viewing stars.
- Take a walk.
- Ride your bike to work.
- Explore local parks.
- Go camping.
- Bring nature indoors with living plants.
- Set limits on screen time for your children, and encourage more green time.
- Mount a bird feeder.
- Climb a tree.
- Vacation in nearby state parks.
- Picnic outside regularly in good weather.
- Go hiking on the Sabbath with family and friends.
- Sleep outside under the stars.
- Go sailing or canoeing.
- Swim in a river or lake.
- Pick up trash in your neighborhood.
- Plant trees.
- Support open spaces and green corridors.
- Let your backyard "go wild."
- Sit outside and journal in one spot throughout the seasons.

- Explore the edges of places—hedgerows, forests, pastures, streambeds.
- Learn the name of every tree in your neighborhood.
- Learn to identify the birds that live in your neighborhood and how they change with the seasons.
- Start or expand a garden, using no fertilizers or pesticides.
- Pick fruit in local orchards in season.
- STOP and watch the sun rise and the sun set, whenever possible.

Adapted with permission from Go Green, Save Green: A Simple Guide to Saving Time, Money and God's Green Earth *(Nancy Sleeth, Tyndale, 2009). For more ideas, visit www.blessedearth.org.*

EIGHT

The First Environmental Music
The Psalms

Praise him, sun and moon; praise him, all you shining stars!

Praise him, you highest heavens, and you waters above the heavens!

Let them praise the name of the Lord, for he commanded and they were created.

He established them forever and ever; he fixed their bounds, which cannot be passed.

Praise the Lord from the earth, you sea monsters and all deeps,

fire and hail, snow and frost, stormy wind fulfilling his command!

Mountains and all hills, fruit trees and all cedars!

Wild animals and all cattle, creeping things and flying birds!

(Ps. 148)

I first met Randy where I meet a lot of people: in the ER. He was being admitted to the hospital, and his internist had asked me to "tuck him in." He had cancer, which he'd been battling for years. In every way he was a pleasant gentleman, the sort of person who gives back even in illness. The subject of our conversation turned to art, music, and literature. He had been hospitalized on numerous occasions and always brought something to read and music to listen to. On this day, however, he had left his books and music at home. I lent him the book I was reading as well as the CD player I carried and some music. It was the start of a friendship.

Randy loved to sing. He'd started out at the Blackhawk restaurant in Chicago, when he was in college. Later, he'd sung with Chick Webb's orchestra beside Ella Fitzgerald at the Savoy in Harlem. When I met Randy, he was leading a swing band with thirty members; he also ran a music store and hosted a weekly FM jazz show. But Randy knew he was losing his battle with cancer, so he scheduled one last concert at the local arts theater. In the weeks leading up to the performance, I got to know him better. We met for breakfast and listened to vinyl records. My best medical guess was that he wouldn't make it to his last show. He was hospitalized just days before the concert.

The day of the concert arrived, and Randy was released from the hospital. Nancy and I attended. When the band started playing, Randy appeared gaunt and tired, and then he came to the microphone and sang a duet with a young colleague. It was as if someone flipped a light switch. His entire body became animated. Illness and the years slipped away; his voice enthralled the audience for more than an hour. We all knew it was his last performance. The song I recall most vividly is an old tune about domestic bliss: "My Blue Heaven." We all had a piece of heaven while he sang. Randy passed away a few days later.

What does music have to do with caring for God's creation? According to the Bible, a lot. In fact, one whole book of the Bible—one hundred and fifty psalms—is devoted to music. And one of the most prevalent themes throughout the psalms is the beauty of God's

> **From ancient times, God's Word has been received with music and song.**
>
> *"All Israel brought up the ark of the covenant of the LORD with shouting, to the sound of the horn, trumpets, and cymbals, and made loud music on harps and lyres" (1 Chron. 15:28).*

creation. The psalms are the world's first collection of environmental worship music.

Nancy and I recently went through the psalms, underlining everything that has to do with caring for creation, celebrating creation, God's revealing himself through creation, and the language of creation. Although I had always known the psalms were filled with environmental lyrics, I was pretty astonished to find references to God's creation in nearly half of the psalms.

From Psalm 1, where a righteous person is compared to "trees planted along the riverbank, bearing fruit each season" to Psalm 150 where we are called to praise God with cymbals and tambourines for all "his mighty works," the Psalms are God's Green Book.

I have loved music ever since I can remember. If there were one thing that electricity could do—and nothing else—I would keep it for music. Cynics may poke barbs at images of harps in heaven: why would someone want to float around for all eternity plucking strings? The answer is that music is the ethereal element. It represents pure contentment and beauty. It may be as close to heaven as we can get on this side of the veil.

Augustine defined a *sacrament* as "a visible sign of an invisible reality." A modern layperson's definition of a *sacrament* is when we take hold of something and God takes hold of the other end. Music is not usually listed among the sacraments (i.e., baptism, communion), but I wonder if it shouldn't be.

If the Bible were written today, I believe that it probably would have a button to push for music. Music—the stuff that floats across the air and vibrates our tympanic membranes—is about as close

---

Music is a way to celebrate the Lord's blessings and offer thanks.

*"The priests stood at their posts; the Levites also, with the instruments for music to the L*ORD *that King David had made for giving thanks to the L*ORD*—for his steadfast love endures forever" (2 Chron. 7:6).*

to transcendent as something can be. Played at the proper levels, it doesn't make one tired, stupid, or overweight. It isn't bad for the heart or cholesterol. It can be made for free. Like the face of a spouse or child, it can be remembered with astonishing detail, yet hearing it (like seeing a loved one in the flesh) is infinitely superior.

The Bible contains songs about every topic imaginable. Moses sings when delivered from slavery (Exod. 15:1), all the Hebrews sing thanks for water in the desert (Num. 21:17), and Deborah's song celebrates victory over the enemy (Judg. 5:24–27). Song of Solomon is a song about love. Mary sings about conception in the song named the Magnificat (Luke 1:46–55). Yet no theme is more prevalent in the music of Scripture than God's creation. The songs most commonly associated with creation care are Psalms 23, 24, 69, 104, 107, and 148.

Psalm 24:1–2 is a clarion call of truth, *"The earth is the LORD's and all that is in it, the world, and those who live in it; for he has founded it on the seas, and established it on the rivers."* The order of the cosmos is established. The earth is the Lord's, and we—along with "all" that is in the environment—belong to its creator. This truth is not the human-centered (anthropocentric) universe of our times. Rather, it is one in which, *"The heavens declare the glory of God, the skies proclaim the work of his hands"* (Ps. 19:1, NIV).

The exuberance of the psalms and the psalmists is tangible as it speaks of the excitement of nature, *"Let the heavens be glad, and let the earth rejoice; let the sea roar, and all that fills it; let the field exalt, and everything in it. Then shall all the trees of the forest sing for joy before the LORD; for he is coming, for he is coming to judge the earth"* (Ps. 96:11–13). The sea, trees, and the field are not relegated to the

> **Music is a way to lift us up and connect with the transcendence of God.**
>
> *"Whenever the evil spirit from God came upon Saul, David took the lyre and played it with his hand, and Saul would be relieved and feel better, and the evil spirit would depart from him"* (1 Sam. 16:23).

status of mere real estate whose sole purpose is for the transactions of mankind. Nature, the psalmist would imply, is the harbinger of the Lord.

Psalm 104 is a tour de force of the natural world. I will not attempt to analyze it. I let it speak for all its wild and glorious self:

Bless the LORD, O my soul. O LORD my God, you are very great.

You are clothed with honor and majesty, wrapped in light as with a garment.

You stretch out the heavens like a tent, you set the beams of your chambers on the waters,

you make the clouds your chariot, you ride on the wings of the wind,

you make the winds your messengers, fire and flame your ministers.

You set the earth on its foundations, so that it shall never be shaken.

You cover it with the deep as with a garment; the waters stood above the mountains.

At your rebuke they flee; at the sound of your thunder they take to flight.

They rose up to the mountains, ran down to the valleys to the place that you appointed for them.

You set a boundary that they may not pass, so that they might not again cover the earth.

Music can awaken the spirit—"Awake, my soul! Awake, O harp and lyre! I will awake the dawn" *(Ps. 57:8)* **and fill us with gratitude—** *"Praise the LORD with the lyre; make melody to him with the harp of ten strings" (Ps. 33:2). "I will also praise you with the harp for your faithfulness, O my God; I will sing praises to you with the lyre, O Holy One of Israel" (Ps. 71:22).*

You make springs gush forth in the valleys; they flow between the hills,

giving drink to every wild animal; the wild asses quench their thirst.

By the streams the birds of the air have their habitation; they sing among the branches.

From your lofty abode you water the mountains; the earth is satisfied with the fruit of your work.

You cause the grass to grow for the cattle, and plants for people to use, to bring forth food from the earth,

and wine to gladden the human heart, oil to make the face shine, and bread to strengthen the human heart.

The trees of the LORD are watered abundantly, the cedars of Lebanon that he planted.

In them the birds build their nests; the stork has its home in the fir trees.

The high mountains are for the wild goats; the rocks are a refuge for the coneys.

You have made the moon to mark the seasons; the sun knows its time for setting.

You make darkness, and it is night, when all the animals of the forest come creeping out.

The young lions roar for their prey, seeking their food from God.

When the sun rises, they withdraw and lie down in their dens.

Music is a form of celebration.

"Sing aloud to God our strength; shout for joy to the God of Jacob. Raise a song, sound the tambourine, the sweet lyre with the harp. Blow the trumpet at the new moon, at the full moon, on our festal day" (Ps. 81:1–3).

People go out to their work and to their labor until the evening.

O LORD, how manifold are your works! In wisdom you have made them all; the earth is full of your creatures.

Yonder is the sea, great and wide, creeping things innumerable are there, living things both small and great.

There go the ships, and Leviathan that you formed to sport in it.

These all look to you to give them their food in due season;

when you give to them, they gather it up; when you open your hand, they are filled with good things.

When you hide your face, they are dismayed; when you take away their breath, they die and return to their dust.

When you send forth your spirit, they are created; and you renew the face of the ground.

May the glory of the LORD endure forever; may the LORD rejoice in his works—

who looks on the earth and it trembles, who touches the mountains and they smoke.

I will sing to the LORD as long as I live; I will sing praise to my God while I have being.

May my meditation be pleasing to him, for I rejoice in the LORD.

Let sinners be consumed from the earth, and let the wicked be no more. Bless the LORD, O my soul. Praise the LORD!

Music is an expression of joyful praise.

"Praise the LORD! Sing to the LORD a new song, his praise in the assembly of the faithful. Let Israel be glad in its Maker; let the children of Zion rejoice in their King. Let them praise his name with dancing, making melody to him with tambourine and lyre. For the LORD takes pleasure in his people; he adorns the humble with victory. Let the faithful exult in glory; let them sing for joy" (Ps. 149:1–5).

Psalm 104 is among the great green hymns of old, but what of the modern world? One of the oldest "new" songs in the hymnal will celebrate its eight hundredth anniversary in a few years. It is the *Cantico di fratre sole*, or Song of Brother Sun, more commonly known as "All Creatures of Our God and King" by the patron saint of the environment, St. Francis of Assisi.

> All creatures of our God and King,
> lift up your voices, let us sing:
> Alleluia, alleluia!
> Thou burning sun with golden beams,
> thou silver moon that gently gleams,
> Refrain:
> O praise him, O praise him,
> Alleluia, alleluia, alleluia!
>
> Thou rushing wind that art so strong,
> ye clouds that sail in heaven along,
> O praise him, Alleluia!
> Thou rising morn, in praise rejoice,
> ye lights of evening, find a voice, (R)
>
> Thou flowing water, pure and clear,
> make music for thy Lord to hear,
> Alleluia, alleluia!

Generation after generation, we have sung our praises to God for the "works of his hand."

"It is good to give thanks to the LORD, to sing praises to your name, O Most High; to declare your steadfast love in the morning, and your faithfulness by night, to the music of the lute and the harp, to the melody of the lyre" (Ps. 92:1–3).

Thou fire so masterful and bright,
that givest man both warmth and light, (R)

Dear mother earth, who day by day
unfoldest blessings on our way,
O praise him, Alleluia!
The flowers and fruits that in thee grow,
let them his glory also show: (R)

And all ye men of tender heart,
forgiving others, take your part,
O sing ye Alleluia!
Ye who long pain and sorrow bear,
praise God and on him cast your care: (R)

And thou, most kind and gentle death,
waiting to hush our latest breath,
O praise him, Alleluia!
Thou leadest home the child of God,
and Christ our Lord the way hath trod: (R)

Let all things their Creator bless,
and worship him in humbleness,
O praise him, Alleluia!
Praise, praise the Father, praise the Son,
and praise the Spirit, Three in One: (R)

Music echoes the beauty of God's creation.

"Make a joyful noise to the Lord, all the earth; break forth into joyous song and sing praises. . . . Let the sea roar, and all that fills it; the world and those who live in it. Let the floods clap their hands; let the hills sing together for joy at the presence of the Lord" (Ps. 98:4, 7–9).

Many hymns written since Francis of Assisi connect the love of the Creator with the creation, including:

- "This Is My Father's World"
- "For the Beauty of the Earth"
- "America the Beautiful"
- "Hymn of Promise"
- "All Things Bright and Beautiful"
- "Beautiful Savior"
- "The Doxology"
- "For the Beauty of the Earth"
- "For the Healing of the Nations"
- "God Who Made the Earth"
- "God Who Touchest Earth with Beauty"
- "I Sing the Mighty Power of God"
- "Immortal, Invisible, God Only Wise"
- "Joyful, Joyful We Adore Thee"
- "Let All Things Now Living"
- "Morning Has Broken"
- "Not Here for High and Holy Things"
- "Now the Green Blade Riseth"

Music fills our hearts with thanksgiving for the world God created to sustain us.

"Sing to the LORD with thanksgiving; make melody to our God on the lyre. He covers the heavens with clouds, prepares rain for the earth, makes grass grow on the hills. He gives to the animals their food, and to the young ravens when they cry" (Ps. 147:7–9).

- "O All Ye Works of God"
- "Psalm 104"
- "Saint Patrick's Breastplate"
- "The Spacious Firmament on High"
- "The Works of the Lord Are Created in Wisdom"
- "'Tis the Gift to Be Simple"
- "We Plow the Fields, and Scatter"

One of my favorite modern musicians to break through with a message that connects "green" and "Bible" was born in Washington, DC, and raised with a hybrid of Orthodox Judaism and Pentecostalism. He began his musical career as a drummer, played percussion on the 1961 Marvelettes' hit, "Please Mr. Postman," and helped write "Dancing in the Streets." His album *What's Going On* garnered national attention in 1971. It contains one of my favorite environmental songs, "Mercy, Mercy Me (The Ecology)."

Woo mercy, mercy me, things ain't what they use to be no no
   Oil wasted on the ocean and our seas and fish full of mercury. . . .

The winds with hymns of praise are loud,
Or low with sobs of pain,—
The thunder-organ of the cloud,
The dropping tears of rain.
The blue sky is the temple's arch,
Its transept earth and air,
The music of its starry march
The chorus of a prayer.
                    The Complete Poetical Works of John Greenleaf Whittier,
                        John Greenleaf Whittier (1807–1892)

The last refrain of the song is, "My sweet Lord, my sweet Lord." The artist is Marvin Gaye, whose life, like those of many gifted artists throughout the ages, was troubled and dogged by tragedy. Yet his album contains songs about pollution, crime, corruption—and God. "Jesus left us a long time ago; He left us a book to believe in," Gaye crooned in his three-octave voice. Singing about the environment and God is as old as the Bible. Marvin Gaye was following a five-thousand-year-old tradition established in the book of Psalms.

Music is one of many tools that communities of faith can bring to the great struggles that face humanity. Some of the tools we offer are the same as the secular world's, but our tradition of song is without substitute. It is in singing that I find the greatest and, by human terms, the most inexplicable hope. What does a song really accomplish? In a way, perhaps, hymns are a sacrament, and as such they are infused with more than we can understand by mere philosophy.

I am not a great speaker. I have trouble staying on track or reducing concepts to sound bites. I am not a spokesperson for Christ so much as a fool for him. If there is a reason I'm invited to speak at so many places, it is perhaps because of the novelty of someone getting up and telling the truth about God's love for his creation—without anything to gain.

I found myself in that situation this past summer. I was at a conference on faith and the environment. On the last day during a question-and-answer session, a young girl about twelve years old raised her hand and asked *the* question.

"Is it too late to save the planet?" she wanted to know.

And hark! how blithe the throstle sings!
He, too, is no mean preacher;
Come forth into the light of things;
*   Let Nature be your teacher.*

Complete Works, "Up, Up My Friend," *London,*
William Wordsworth (1770–1850)

If I had been asked this before I became a Christian, I would have answered, "Yes—it's too late." But that is not what I answer today, despite much logic that points in a fatalistic direction. No, I do not believe it is too late, though we need to start making changes now. I base my answer on personal history. In my lifetime, people have made what seemed at the time impossible changes. And music was very much front and center.

Let me illustrate: when I was little, we learned a song called "Jesus Loves the Little Children."

Jesus loves the little children,
all the children of the world,
Red and yellow, black and white
they are precious in his sight
Jesus loves the little children of the world.

When I first learned that song in the late 1950s, the song did not seem true in the real world. Segregation still existed. My uncle and aunt wanted to marry at the end of the Second World War—but an interracial marriage was against the law in the state in which they lived. They had to travel to the District of Columbia to marry.

> *If for a moment you are inclined to regard these talus slopes as mere draggled, chaotic dumps, climb to the top of one of them, tie your mountain shoes firmly over the instep, and with braced nerves run down without any haggling, puttering hesitation, boldly jumping from boulder to boulder with even speed. You will then find your feet playing a tune, and quickly discover the music and poetry of rock piles—a fine lesson; and all Nature's wildness tells the same story. Storms of every sort, torrents, earthquakes, cataclysms, "convulsions of nature," etc., are only harmonious notes in the song of creation, varied expressions of God's love.*
>
> My First Summer in the Sierras, *John Muir (1838–1914)*

Jesus loved my biracial cousins, but some people didn't. Still, millions of us learned to sing about Jesus' loving all the children of the world. We sang in hope. We sang what was true in a sacramental sense. Jesus always loved the little children. Eventually the country changed, and although it may not be perfect regarding race, the United States has elected a biracial president, which would have seemed impossible to my aunt and uncle.

I heard children singing another song of hope a year ago. I was visiting a college on a mountain overlooking the Napa Valley. Before my chapel talk, a visiting elementary-school class got up and sang a few songs. The class was populated by every color and ethnic group on the planet. To the children, teachers, and the audience, color was a nonissue. This change that has swept over the land in the last half century seemed unattainable at the start, yet it has in large part been accomplished. In the minds of people who live in other countries, religious, racial, and ethnic tolerance is one of the finest qualities our country has to offer.

On the day of the chapel, the children were not singing about racial equality. They sang about something that seems equally improbable—cleaning up the world. The refrain of the song was: "I can clean up the earth, with my two hands." The message seems as likely as everyone loving all the little children of the world in 1956, or "We shall overcome" in 1856. But music has a way of inspiring and moving us toward "outward signs of invisible truths."

> *Like a musician who has tuned his lyre, and by the artistic blending of low and high and medium tones produces a single melody, so the Wisdom of God, holding the universe like a lyre, adapting things heavenly to things earthly, and earthly things to heavenly, harmonizes them all, and leading them by His will, makes one world and one world order in beauty and harmony.*
>
> Contra Gentes, in George Maloney, S.J., The Cosmic Christ,
> St. Athanasius (c. 297–373)

If I had large sums of money to save the world, I'd hold a "Blessed Earth" music festival and have a million believers sing their hearts out to God, clapping their hands alongside the psalmists' trees. I believe in the power of music to change the world, God's world. So did the psalmist who wrote the first environmental worship music. Singing songs in praise of creation inspires us to appreciate God's gifts. Appreciation leads to a desire to be better stewards. Better stewardship at home, church, work, and beyond leads to less waste. Less waste demonstrates respect for God, resulting in a cleaner, more beautiful world in which to sing his praises.

I once saw music bring a man at death's door back to life for one more concert.

With God as the conductor, maybe music can also save a planet.

Delightful would it be to me
to be in Uchd Ailiun [an Irish headland over the sea]
On the pinnacle of a rock,
That I might often see the face of the ocean;
That I might see its heaving waves over the wide ocean,
When they chant music to their Father upon the world's course.
Songs of Columba, *St. Columba (521–597)*

Tending the Garden
What you can do to celebrate God's gifts of music and the arts

- Ask your church to sing some of the hymns listed in this chapter.

- If you are a musician or singer, learn creation-care songs and share them with others.

- Compose your own creation-care songs (we heard a beautiful original song by a young lady at church a couple of weeks ago); record your songs and use them to ignite a revival.

- Write poems celebrating God's creation.

- Make a video about the glories of creation and what we can do to help preserve it.

- Even if you are not a "talented artist," sit outside and draw a favorite tree through the seasons.

- Write a play for your youth group about what we can do to care for creation.

- Get creative: make art from "found" objects, reusing discarded materials.

- Go to an art museum with your children, and look closely at landscapes from a century or more ago. Look at the height and breadth of the trees. Examine the clarity of the stars, the unpolluted waters, the fields minus the strip malls. Discuss what has changed in the landscape since the painter took this "photo" on canvas. What are some of the differences between a God-made world and a man-made world?

- Digital cameras make photography accessible to everyone. Create a photo-documentary exhibit, seeing your neighborhood through God's eyes. Or hold a creation-care-themed photo contest at your church or school. Post the photographs on the Web.

- If you are an artist, look for ways to green up your artwork. Can you use less toxic materials? Can you recycle material, or reuse materials?

- Write a short story with a creation-care theme.

- Write a personal essay, sharing your creation-care journey and send to contact@blessedearth.org.

- Keep a journal. Note the changes in the seasons, what wildlife comes and goes in your neighborhood. How much time do people spend outdoors? When do the stars seem the brightest? Where does the sun rise and set? How high in the sky is the sun at noon? When does each wildflower bloom? When do the leaves first bud, and when do the first leaves change color? What color is most prevalent first in the fall foliage? The first naturalists were mostly ministers. They understood the connection between God's creation and the need to celebrate and observe its glory. You can, too—a great way to engage your children in green time rather than screen time.

Adapted with permission from Go Green, Save Green: A Simple Guide to Saving Time, Money and God's Green Earth *(Nancy Sleeth, Tyndale, 2009). For more ideas, visit www.blessedearth.org.*

NINE

Food
Daniel

Daniel resolved that he would not defile himself with the royal
rations of food and wine; so he asked the palace master to
allow him not to defile himself. Now God allowed Daniel to
receive favor and compassion from the palace master. The
palace master said to Daniel, "I am afraid of my lord the king;
he has appointed your food and your drink. If he should see you
in poorer condition than the other young men of your own age,
you would endanger my head with the king." Then Daniel asked
the guard whom the palace master had appointed over Daniel,
Hananiah, Mishael, and Azariah: "Please test your servants for
ten days. Let us be given vegetables to eat and water to drink.
You can then compare our appearance with the appearance of
the young men who eat the royal rations, and deal with your
servants according to what you observe." So he agreed to this
proposal and tested them for ten days. At the end of ten days it
was observed that they appeared better and fatter than all the
young men who had been eating the royal rations. So the guard
continued to withdraw their royal rations and the wine they
were to drink, and gave them vegetables. *(Dan. 1:8–16)*

If you are looking for big adventure, reversals of fortune, and
miracles galore, then the book of Daniel is one to read. Even those
who've never studied Daniel are familiar with phrases like "feet of

clay" and "clear as the writing on the wall." The story begins when Judea is sacked by the Babylonians in 587 B.C. Daniel and his three friends are marched five hundred miles to the Euphrates River to the palace of King Nebuchadnezzar. There they face various trials ranging from time in a lions' den to a session in a blazing industrial brick oven. Daniel talks with angels, interprets the king's dreams, and lives to see the fall of Babylon to the Medo-Persian Empire in 539 B.C.—and all this happened because he followed his mother's advice and ate his vegetables.

In the Babylonian palace, Daniel faced the hard task of surviving while keeping his faith. Imagine the difficulty of maintaining spiritual and intellectual integrity in the capture of a hostile enemy. Yet, Daniel lived out his faith under these circumstances—as have the Hebrew people through much of their history.

Daniel's first act of independence involves food. He is determined to follow the dietary rules of his faith, so he declines the royal rations. Because Daniel wishes not to defile himself, God allows him to find favor with the palace master. The palace master is sympathetic, but worried: *"I am afraid of my lord the king; he has appointed your food and your drink. If he should see you in poorer condition than the other young men of your own age, you would endanger my head with the king."* So Daniel strikes a deal. Allow Daniel and his three friends to eat only vegetables and drink only water for ten days. Then compare their fitness with the men who have been given the royal rations. If Daniel and his three friends look worse, then the palace master can do with them what he wishes. The palace master

---

God produced a wide variety of foods to sustain all humanity.

"God said, 'Let the earth put forth vegetation: plants yielding seed, and fruit trees of every kind on earth that bear fruit with the seed in it.' And it was so. The earth brought forth vegetation: plants yielding seed of every kind, and trees of every kind bearing fruit with the seed in it. And God saw that it was good" (Gen. 1:11–12).

agrees. Ten days later, he finds Daniel and his friends appearing more fit than all the young men who had been eating the royal rations (Dan. 1:8–15).

Biblical scholars commonly give two reasons why Daniel refused the rich palace food. The first is that he and his friends understood that to accept—and therefore grow accustomed to the palace food—was the first step to becoming fully assimilated into the Babylonian way of life. This way of life not only included food that was prohibited under Jewish law but also the worship of gods other than the God of Abraham, Isaac, and Jacob. In this sense Daniel and his friends appreciated that becoming a slave not only involves forced labor, such as making bricks when the Hebrews were held captive in Egypt; slavery can also be accomplished through the unquestioning acceptance of luxury.

The second reason these Judean captives refused the royal rations is because they were forbidden by the laws given in the book of Leviticus. We commonly think of the parts of the law that forbid the eating of pork, shellfish, and scavengers. But the agricultural laws practiced by the Hebrews for thousands of years go beyond not

At every meal, we can choose foods that honor God's creation or foods that dishonor him.

"Daniel asked the guard whom the palace master had appointed over Daniel, Hananiah, Mishael, and Azariah: 'Please test your servants for ten days. Let us be given vegetables to eat and water to drink. You can then compare our appearance with the appearance of the young men who eat the royal rations, and deal with your servants according to what you observe.' So he agreed to this proposal and tested them for ten days. At the end of ten days it was observed that they appeared better and fatter than all the young men who had been eating the royal rations. So the guard continued to withdraw their royal rations and the wine they were to drink, and gave them vegetables" (Dan. 1:11–16).

eating milk with meat. They are designed to ensure the protection and preservation of:

- The land itself
- The animals used in domestic work
- The animals used as livestock
- Wildlife
- Indigent peoples
- Future generations
- The health and well-being of the believer who is consuming food

Most Americans today do not suffer from lack of food. I say this knowing that many in our land have little food security and will go hungry today. However, more often we face the temptation of too much—the enticement that Daniel encountered.

For the most part, the richness and abundance of food available to us, not the lack of it, causes harm. In America, four hundred thousand people weigh more than four hundred pounds, and nearly four million Americans weigh more than three hundred pounds. The unhealthy condition of our waistlines is analogous to what is happening in agriculture and nature as a whole. Our appetites for meat, food out of season, and food from exotic places has a detrimental impact on the health of ourselves and the planet.

When we look to the wisdom contained in the book of Daniel, the first thing we note is that Daniel and his friends suffered no

> **One way we can honor God's sustaining gifts is to eat simply so that others—even our enemies—may simply eat.**
>
> *"If your enemies are hungry, give them bread to eat; and if they are thirsty, give them water to drink" (Prov. 25:21).*

ill effects from their diet of vegetables. Today, I need hardly make an argument that a food plan that focuses on fruits and vegetables would do our country good. If adopted by all, the rates of coronary artery disease, gout, osteoarthritis, and Type 2 diabetes would all plummet. We should heed the wisdom of Proverbs 25:27, which warns us against eating too much of anything, even honey.

Although I am not a vegetarian, I cannot ignore the fact that God's original plan for humanity was for us to eat only plant life. Perhaps in both a literal and metaphorical sense, God's first warning to humanity is to not eat our way into trouble: *"You may freely eat of every tree of the garden; but of the tree of the knowledge of good and evil you shall not eat, or in the day that you eat of it you shall die"* (Gen. 2:16–17).

I therefore do not find it surprising that God sends his chosen people forward with a detailed set of dietary and agricultural laws. To emphasize the importance of food, a tithe is instituted on the "first fruits" of grain, wine, oil, herds, flocks, and seeds (Deut. 14:22–23). The first portion of agriculture belongs to God. Further, God's people have an understanding that the land is not to be exhausted—it is not okay to get as much from every acre as a farmer possibly can. The land is to be left fallow at regular intervals—every seven years, the Sabbath year. This is why God instructs his people not to harvest to the edge of their fields, not to pick up dropped fruit, and not to beat olive trees twice. Instead, the Hebrew people understand that long-term economic viability is not served by greed

---

When we feed those who are hungry, we are caring for Jesus and sharing his love.

"The king will say to those at his right hand, 'Come, you that are blessed by my Father, inherit the kingdom prepared for you from the foundation of the world; for I was hungry and you gave me food, I was thirsty and you gave me something to drink, I was a stranger and you welcomed me'" (Matt. 25:34–35).

or the worship of efficiency. The Bible presents a case for eating food grown in ways that ensure the long-term health of the land.

Today we assign corporations and individuals rights, but in the Bible land and nature itself are assigned rights. Indeed, *"the earth is the Lord's"* (Exod. 9:29), and God maintains the right to evict dwellers from the land who abuse it (Deut. 29). Although we may be concerned only with ourselves, God takes a multigenerational view of things.

One way that God ensures the long-term health of his land is by calling for a Sabbath rest:

> Six years you shall sow your field, and six years you shall prune your vineyard, and gather in their yield; but in the seventh year there shall be a sabbath of complete rest for the land, a sabbath for the Lord: you shall not sow your field or prune your vineyard. You shall not reap the aftergrowth of your harvest or gather the grapes of your unpruned vine: it shall be a year of complete rest for the land. You may eat what the land yields during its sabbath—you, your male and female slaves, your hired and your bound laborers who live with you; for

---

Feeding others is a form of compassion.

"Jesus called his disciples to him and said, 'I have compassion for the crowd, because they have been with me now for three days and have nothing to eat; and I do not want to send them away hungry, for they might faint on the way.'. . .

"He took the seven loaves and the fish; and after giving thanks he broke them and gave them to the disciples, and the disciples gave them to the crowds.

"And all of them ate and were filled; and they took up the broken pieces left over, seven baskets full. Those who had eaten were four thousand men, besides women and children" (Matt. 15:32, 36–38).

your livestock also, and for the wild animals in your land all its yield shall be for food. (Lev. 25:4–7)

Thus the land, wild animals, domestic creatures, the poor, and immigrants are protected by proper care for the land. Contrast this Sabbath practice to the modern portrayal of agribusiness where corporations are literally allowed to patent life. Even a cursory investigation of genetically modified seeds and factory-raised livestock offers food for thought as to the morality of supporting a system of agriculture that does not heed God.

Perhaps the best known of all biblical instruction about animal care is found in Deuteronomy 25:4, *"You shall not muzzle an ox while it is treading out the grain."* God states that it would be cruel to have one of his creatures helping to make grain and deny the beast a taste of it. The practice of letting the working ox eat the grain it was grinding represented a significant economic toll for the farmer. Nonetheless, godly agriculture is not about short-term profits and pleasing shareholders. It's about pleasing the Creator of the universe.

Entire books have been devoted to a full discussion of the agricultural and dietary laws under which Israel lived. What it boils down to is that God wants us to treat all of his creation lovingly, as he does. Indeed, the book of Proverbs (12:10) assigns the quality of "righteousness" to one who understands the needs of animals. Deuteronomy 22 tells us that if we happen upon a bird sitting upon eggs or its young, we are prohibited from taking the nesting bird. One who follows this instruction is reassured by a blessing that "it may

When we defile God's land through factory farming, unnecessary pesticides, and overuse of fertilizers, we show disrespect for his creation.

"I brought you into a plentiful land to eat its fruits and its good things. But when you entered you defiled my land, and made my heritage an abomination" (Jer. 2:7).

be well with you and that you may prolong your days." As Jesus said, we have the kind of God who groans when a single sparrow falls from the sky.

One biblical concept that flies in the face of modern factory farming is that of not insulting the animal one is eating. For instance, under Jewish law, meat is not served in the milk of its mother (Exod. 23:19). By contrast, factory farming regularly employs the practice of feeding cows, pigs, and chickens the ground up remains of their parents and other animals, irrespective of whether or not God designed the animal as an herbivore. In factory farms, an animal may be kept in a cage where it will never be able to see the light of day, turn around, lie down, walk, or fly. As is seen in the Levitical laws, the use of animals for food is allowed, but they must be treated with respect. We are all God's creatures.

By contrast, in modern factory farming, speed and the bottom line are all that count. One example is the way that modern cattle are raised. To speed up the "finishing" phase of their short (fourteen-month) life, feed lots insert a plastic implant that releases estrogen into the ears of beef cattle. The implant costs less than two dollars and can result in a steer gaining forty extra pounds. The cost to the cattle owner is minimal, but the cost to society may be enormous in terms of increased breast cancers, early onset of puberty, and changes in male characteristics—in both humans and other species affected by manure runoff and water contamination.

> **God wants us to depend on him, not on unhealthy cravings, worries, or addictions.**
>
> *"I tell you, do not worry about your life, what you will eat or what you will drink, or about your body, what you will wear. Is not life more than food, and the body more than clothing?*
>
> *"Look at the birds of the air; they neither sow nor reap nor gather into barns, and yet your heavenly Father feeds them. Are you not of more value than they?" (Matt. 6:25–26).*

Consumers can make an ethical choice at the supermarket: paying a couple of dollars more for a steak not raised on hormones and antibiotics is better for you and the earth. And that extra cost can easily be offset by purchasing smaller cuts of meat, or eating one extra meatless meal per week. Yet the vast majority of meat purchased in the United States is full of these harmful hormones; in Europe and other countries, the practice of raising beef on supplemental female sex hormones is considered so harmful to both humans and other animals that it has been outlawed.

When considering how we feed and house animals, we should remember that Christ was born among farm animals. He spent his first night in a manger. Jesus is often called the Good Shepherd. The first visitors to attend him took care of sheep.

While it is true that the New Covenant releases Christ's followers from ancient dietary restrictions, we are still commanded to be good stewards of the earth and to show our love for God by caring for our neighbors. In Acts 10, Peter goes up on a roof, with the sun high overhead, to pray. His stomach growls, and he falls into a trance. He sees a vision of a sheet being lowered from heaven. On the sheet are all manner of unclean or nonkosher animals. Peter is commanded by God to eat all the animals. At first Peter objects. He has never broken the Levitical dietary laws. God answers: *Look, I make the rules—if I say eat anything, then I mean eat anything.* At first, Peter

---

Indeed, God is the wine and the milk and the very living waters that bring life.

"Ho, everyone who thirsts, come to the waters; and you that have no money, come, buy and eat! Come, buy wine and milk without money and without price.

"Why do you spend your money for that which is not bread, and your labor for that which does not satisfy? Listen carefully to me, and eat what is good, and delight yourselves in rich food" (Isa. 55:1–2).

is puzzled by the vision. Then two servants of a Roman centurion arrive at the house where Peter is staying and bid him to visit their master, Cornelius.

The following day, Peter journeys to the home of Cornelius. There, the meaning of the vision becomes clear to Peter, and he declares, "*You yourselves know that it is unlawful for a Jew to associate with or to visit a Gentile; but God has shown me that I should not call anyone profane or unclean*" (Acts 10:28). At last! The great barrier between Jew and Gentile is dissolved. Peter not only enters the house of the Roman Gentile, but he preaches, teaches, baptizes them, and eats with him. Later, Peter receives grief from Christ's Jewish followers for eating the unclean food of a Gentile. There must have been considerable controversy about the kosher laws and Peter's assertion that all foods are now clean. To resolve the disagreement, the first church council is called in Jerusalem.

After much discussion, James gives the judgment that the Gentiles need only abstain from sexual immorality, meat that is strangled, meat sacrificed to idols, and blood from animals.

The words of James still apply to you and me today. Over the past several years I have been taken out to eat hundreds of times. At nearly every meal, I have observed one self-imposed dietary rule: I order what the person across from me gets. In a world of divisions and loneliness, I think it's more important for me to build fellowship than to choose exactly what I want to eat. The privilege of being relieved of dietary restrictions allows me to eat whatever my neighbor is eating. I do, however, appreciate when people make healthful food choices, and I am thankful if they choose a restaurant that treats their employees well—which often seems to parallel a restaurant's

---

The food that God offers leads to eternal life.

"I am the living bread that came down from heaven. Whoever eats of this bread will live forever; and the bread that I will give for the life of the world is my flesh" (John 6:51).

concern about purchasing food locally or food that is grown without the aid of hormones, antibiotics, and pesticides.

Because we believe that building community is important, Nancy tries to purchase food cooperatively. The meat in our freezer is from a cow named Wendell. Wendell was raised in Lexington close to our home. He never saw a feed lot, antibiotics, or hormones. Because he was grass fed, no oil was used to grow, fertilize, or apply pesticides to Wendell's feed. Wendell converted nondigestable starches in grass to edible proteins in an operation that was completely solar powered.

If our guests don't want to eat Wendell, Nancy is ever too happy to make a vegetarian meal. We grow food with our neighbors and buy what we can locally. These days it seems as if anyone can obtain eggs from local backyard hens. Ours come from the janitor of a nearby church. The route from backyard chicken to scrambled eggs also bypasses the complex chemistry of most modern processed foods. What does Amaranth (Red #2), a synthetic dye once prevalent in many foods, really do to the mitochondria in your liver? Maybe it's better that we get our flour from the Amish farmers a few towns over who don't add azodicarbonamide to make our flour look "cleaner." Here's my bottom line for safe eating: If you can't pronounce it, don't eat it.

Because I'm a doctor, people often ask me for dietary advice. One of the most frequent areas of concern is genetically modified organisms (GMOs). The Bible says nothing about splicing fish genes into tomato plants. It does mention grafting, but grafting—unlike genetic engineering—is a process that does not change the genetic structure of an organism. Moreover, the Bible does speak of "like begetting like" and all of life belonging to God (Ps. 24), which would certainly seem to preclude the patenting of food by individuals and corporations.

> *Do not for the sake of food destroy the work of God.*
> *St. Clement of Alexandria (c. 150–c. 215)*

How can a corporation own a gene or a plant if all life belongs to God? The Bible declares repeatedly that everything on earth is God's; we are only sojourners: *"The heavens are yours, the earth also is yours; the world and all that is in it—you have founded them"* (Ps. 89:11).

When I am asked about food issues, I find it helpful to remember that Jesus started his ministry by going into the wilderness for forty days. He was tempted by the devil with all the things that still tempt and seduce humanity today. The last temptation was a call to use the Scriptures and his relationship with God for selfish advantage. This temptation involves our tendency to "test" God.

The second temptation was power and status. If Jesus were alive today, this temptation might involve a camera crew and perhaps an ongoing reality show or book contract.

But Christ's *first* temptation was food. The devil did not tempt Jesus with an all-you-can-eat buffet or a biggy-size burger with special sauce when Christ had missed lunch one day. Rather, the temptation came after a fast lasting *forty* days. Luke, the physician, records that Christ was "famished." Christ's response to the temptation of food was not "I'm lovin' it" but a reminder that "one does not live by bread alone."

The Bible says that if we live for our desires, our minds come to resemble our cravings. By contrast, if we set our minds on spiritual concerns, we obey God because we are not so busy worrying about

---

Christ the Educator, Book II 1–2

The Christian way of life is not achieved by self-indulgence. Far from "lust-exciting delicacies" is the table of truth. . . . It is this goal that provides the strength we need to restrain ourselves from living lives centered around the table. Wealth chooses that sort of life, for its vision is blunted; it is abundance that blinds in the matter of gluttony.

St. Clements of Alexandria (150–220)

our stomachs or satisfying a craving. *"To set the mind on the flesh is death, but to set the mind on the Spirit is life and peace"* (Rom. 8:6).

I like to think of Christ's temptation when I am purchasing and preparing my own food. For most of us, obtaining food that is good for the earth requires extra effort. Daniel went out of his way—even risked the displeasure of the king and thus his life—so that he could obey God's dietary laws. Today in America, where food is cheap and plentiful, it costs us very little to follow the general principles of good stewardship and respect for God's creation.

God does not promise us our quarterly bread. He promises us our daily bread. At least three times a day, we have the opportunity to make choices that harm God's creation or choices that honor him. Instead of having it our way, we all need to begin eating more like Daniel and choose to live God's way.

The produce of the earth is a gift from our gracious Creator to the inhabitants, and to impoverish the earth now to support outward greatness appears to be an injury to the succeeding age.

John Woolman (1720–1772)

Tending the Garden
What you can do to encourage biblical food practices

- Say a prayer before meals, not out of routine but out of genuine thankfulness.
- Read Matthew 15 to be reminded that Christ cares for your physical and nutritional needs.
- Cut back on the amount of meat you eat.
- Replace bottled or canned drinks with tap water.
- Save leftovers instead of throwing them away, and eat them later.
- Visit www.betterworldshopper.org to educate yourself about food companies that you should support.
- Replace restaurant meals with home-cooked meals.
- Purchase cloth grocery bags and use them in place of paper or plastic.
- Shop from a grocery list and avoid impulse purchases.
- Choose organic food over factory farmed.
- Compost food scraps to significantly reduce household waste.
- Buy produce in season.
- Support farmers' markets and small grocers.
- Purchase food in bulk.
- Avoid individually wrapped items.
- Consider how far a food item has traveled before you buy it; find local sources for eggs, honey, meat, and produce.
- Invite friends and strangers to eat in your home.
- Plant a vegetable garden, and share the produce with others.

- Abstain from a less-than-ecologically-sound food during Lent.

- Avoid fast-food restaurants.

- Avoid food packaged in containers that cannot be recycled.

Adapted with permission from Go Green, Save Green: A Simple Guide to Saving Time, Money and God's Green Earth *(Nancy Sleeth, Tyndale, 2009). For more ideas, visit www.blessedearth.org.*

TEN

Community

Acts

They devoted themselves to the apostles' teaching and
fellowship, to the breaking of bread and the prayers. Awe came
upon everyone, because many wonders and signs were being
done by the apostles. All who believed were together and had
all things in common; they would sell their possessions and
goods and distribute the proceeds to all, as any had need. Day
by day, as they spent much time together in the temple, they
broke bread at home and ate their food with glad and generous
hearts, praising God and having the goodwill of all the people.
And day by day the Lord added to their number those who were
being saved. *(Acts 2:42–47)*

I arrived at the Platte Clove Community in the afternoon. My trip
along meandering, nearly deserted roads had been thoroughly enjoy-
able. At frequent intervals, streams crossed under the road, afford-
ing glimpses into the forest. It was the season between late summer
and early fall when the trees bore leaves of green that had neither a
hint of spring nor of turning. The sky was clear except for the con-
trails of a few jets far from landing sites. For some prosperous city
dwellers, these Catskill Mountains are a place to vacation—most of
the second homes I passed stood vacant, maintained to higher stan-
dards than the houses of those who live in the area year-round.

I pulled into a paved drive leading to a cluster of large white buildings. At one time, this community was a summer resort for the New York State police. The trees scattered throughout the grounds have had time to grow and be climbed by children who have long ceased to be children. My first impression was of quiet—no barking dogs, no roar of lawn mowers.

I found my way into what must have once been the lobby and now serves as a reception area. In a welcoming voice, a young man asked if he could help me. He telephoned my friend Milton, then suggested that I might enjoy waiting out on the benches by the oak tree. Within a few minutes, Milton came along, and we shook hands. He is the physician for the three hundred fifty people living in this community. The residents range in age from newborn to more than ninety. Many have lived here all of their lives.

The Platte Clove Community is best known as the *Bruderhof,* German for the "brotherhood." The Bruderhof was started as an intentional Christian community by Eberhard Arnold in Germany before World War II. The Nazis forced the Bruderhof out of Germany, so they fled to England. When the war began, the British asked them to leave, so they sailed to Paraguay. Eventually they made their way to the United States.

The Bruderhof models itself on the first-century church as depicted in the book of Acts—breaking bread together, praying together, and sharing all things in common.

"Sharing all things in common"—an odd concept for our generation. The members of the Bruderhof have no individual money and not much in the way of personal possessions. No one owns an

> **One way that we show our love for God is by reaching out to others in our community.**
>
> *"Religion that is pure and undefiled before God, the Father, is this: to care for orphans and widows in their distress, and to keep oneself unstained by the world" (James 1:27).*

individual car or home. They attempt to live in the love of Jesus, with emphasis on simplicity, family, and lifelong fidelity in marriage. Although there are singles living in the community, the primary social structure is that of the family. Unlike some of the cults that occasionally come to widespread media attention, the Bruderhof community is open to all, and anyone there is free to leave at any time. Couples in the community seem to marry a little later than average—one wife per husband, with people married to others of the same age.

The evening I arrived, the weather was particularly congenial, so the community decided to eat alfresco. People gathered to set up tables, chairs, plates, and food outdoors. With ease and good humor, 350 plates were filled, and the community sat down to eat together. We don't have many places left in society where several hundred people all eat the same thing at the same time. In a "have it your way" world, we do not even eat the same thing at church dinners or around our dinner tables at home. Yet on that evening everyone sat under the blue heavens and ate the same meal, with enough for all. I thought about Jesus' feeding bread and fish to his flock.

The Bruderhof way of life is counterculture in an ancient way. One can board a plane and be in any one of the four corners of the world within a day's time, yet my trip to the Bruderhof in the Catskills of New York seemed to take me further from the prevailing culture of consumerism than a ten-thousand-mile journey.

Watching the community members eat their dinner, I couldn't help noticing that they dress modestly, both in style and in expense. Adult women cover their heads with a scarf, yet they do not appear

---

When we take care of those with less than we have, we are sharing God's love.

"I was hungry and you gave me food, I was thirsty and you gave me something to drink, I was a stranger and you welcomed me, I was naked and you gave me clothing, I was sick and you took care of me, I was in prison and you visited me" (Matt. 25:35–36).

somber; dresses are made of bright prints, and a man might wear plaid, for instance. It is not uncommon to see several women sitting together wearing the exact same outfits, with no discomfort. Individuality in God's eyes runs much deeper than clothes.

"What if someone needs a new watch, or a book?" I asked.

The person in charge of supplies probably has ordered a dozen watches at the same time, I am told. The one needing a new watch would simply be told to pick it up.

"Half the time we ask for a book, we find out that the community already owns a copy."

In the evening, I met with a group of Milton's friends to discuss questions about the church at large and global politics. The group is remarkably well-read. Conversations were not interrupted by cell phones or text messages. The men and women asked thoughtful questions about how they could better care for God's creation, while I asked about their decades of experience living together.

The following day I worked in the community-owned factory, where they manufacture mobility products for handicapped children and adults. I was particularly interested in one man in his mid-twenties. He expressed gratefulness that he could work with his hands alongside his friends and family. "If I were out on my own, I'd probably have to go to college even though I've never been academically inclined. But here my standard of living is exactly the same as it would be if I went to medical school." His observations made me wonder how much of our career choice is based upon income rather than the lifestyle or happiness it provides. If teens here feel a call to go to college, the entire community pays.

Living in community often requires us to put the needs of others before our own desires.

"Do nothing from selfish ambition or conceit, but in humility regard others as better than yourselves. Let each of you look not to your own interests, but to the interests of others" (Phil. 2:3–4).

I toured the large garden, greenhouse, and cutting-edge solar hot-water heating facility. These projects result in fewer resources being used. Certainly the Bruderhof community with its shared possessions, meals, and fortunes is far closer to the standard of the Christian community in Acts than our way of living today.

> The whole group of those who believed were of one heart and soul, and no one claimed private ownership of any possessions, but everything they owned was held in common. With great power the apostles gave their testimony to the resurrection of the Lord Jesus, and great grace was upon them all. There was not a needy person among them, for as many as owned lands or houses sold them and brought the proceeds of what was sold. They laid it at the apostles' feet, and it was distributed to each as any had need.
>
> There was a Levite, a native of Cyprus, Joseph, to whom the apostles gave the name Barnabas (which means "son of encouragement"). He sold a field that belonged to him, then brought the money, and laid it at the apostles' feet. *(Acts 4:32–37)*

The community described in the book of Acts seems idealistic— no poverty, no private ownership, and complete generosity—exactly the type of community that the Broderhof wish to emulate. To some extent they do, indeed, succeed. Certainly they have a lower environmental footprint per person than the average American. I felt that one of the most beguiling facets of their community life is that the frail and elderly are not hidden away in nursing homes. They

---

Inaction is sinful. If we know we can be of help to someone, we must do it, even if it is inconvenient or costly.

"Anyone, then, who knows the right thing to do and fails to do it, commits sin" (James 4:17).

are an integral part of everyday life. I watched with awe when a few eighteen-year-old young men carried a senior and his wheelchair up the hill so he could converse with the young people.

There is a dark side to the Bruderhof's history, and they are open about it. When governance goes wrong in a tightly knit community such as theirs, it can go terribly wrong. But of course this is true even for the governance of a family. It is doubly true for the fractured family.

Yet the desire for Christian communal living goes back centuries and continues in many forms today. St. Anthony is credited with starting the monastic movement in 285 when he was thirty-four years old. Anthony took Christ's advice literally, as recorded in Matthew 19:21: *"If you wish to be perfect, go, sell your possessions, and give the money to the poor, and you will have treasure in heaven; then come, follow me."* Anthony sold all that he had and gave the money to the poor. Then he moved out of town into the Egyptian wilderness. His objective was to live a solitary and simple life of contemplation. He was the first of the desert fathers, although he was certainly not the first to seek God in solitude.

The term *desert father* hints at how *un*successful Anthony was at living the life of a hermit. Before long, pilgrims, politicians, and reporters started showing up at the door to his cave. "No man is an island," as the British poet Donne once wrote. We are creatures of community. Regardless of whether we live in a cave, atop a column, or in the boughs of a redwood tree, the world will seek us out. Eventually Anthony emerged from his hermitage and served as an inspiration to others in his monastic community.

The first-century church gives us a model to strive toward.

"The whole group of those who believed were of one heart and soul, and no one claimed private ownership of any possessions, but everything they owned was held in common" (Acts 4:32).

As humans, we long to belong. Paradoxically, we have fantasies of getting away from it all—of following St. Anthony out into a cabin in the woods, or a shack on a deserted beach.

Can we find a balance between the isolation of St. Anthony, the nonmaterialism of the Bruderhof, and the disconnectedness of our Western society? And can a sense of community lead to a long and fulfilling life? These questions are explored in *The Blue Zones*, where author Dan Buettner examines factors leading to health and longevity. Many of his findings are obvious: people who abstain from tobacco, and who exercise regularly, maintain a reasonable body weight, and avoid large amounts of meat and processed food tend to live longer. But Buettner also found that faith, service to others, a weekly day of rest, minimal TV, Internet, and radio input—as well as time spent in laughter with friends and family—are important parts of the mix. "Healthy centenarians everywhere have faith," says Buettner.

One of the challenges to living in community in our modern society is the frequency and distances that we move. One in six Americans moves every year, and the average American will move nearly twelve times. Our own family is no exception. On the whole, I wish we had stayed put and grown deeper roots in one place. Biblically, the gift of land and place is one of God's great blessings. Homelessness, displacement, and wandering in the desert are less than ideal, but it is the way we live in America. We are a restless people.

My family and I currently live in a small town that has a Christian liberal arts college and a seminary. This mix makes for great transition in the town's population. Yet, most in the town share a common faith.

> **When we intentionally seek to live harmoniously in community, the rewards are abundant.**
>
> *"How very good and pleasant it is when kindred live together in unity!" (Ps. 133:1).*

By comparison, we also have lived in a small town where a majority of the residents resided for multiple generations—but there was no other common thread that bound the townfolk together. Our family has found a much greater sense of community in our transient town of shared faith. Perhaps the sense of belonging in a community is not so much a function of how long one has lived somewhere but of how welcoming the residents are.

In Romans, Paul urges us to offer hospitality to guests, providing them with food and lodging: *"When God's children are in need, be the one to help them out. And get into the habit of inviting guests home for dinner or, if they need lodging, for the night"* (Rom. 12:13, NLT).

I believe that this bit of Scripture is the single best advice about building community. Wherever you live, and for whatever length of time, dig in and love. We need to open our homes and invite others in to fellowship and share a meal.

You may have heard the old joke about an elementary-school teacher discussing various religious traditions with her class. The children were invited to bring in an object symbolizing their faith. The Muslim child brought a prayer rug and explained how it was used in daily prayers. The Jewish child brought a *tallit*, or prayer shawl, and explained why it was worn. Finally the teacher asked the Christian child what he had brought to symbolize his faith. In response, the child held up a casserole dish. Obviously, this youngster was familiar with Romans 12:13.

I did not grow up in a home that offered much in the way of hospitality, and I have learned much from those who open their homes to me—and from my wife, Nancy. She seems to have a natural gift for making people comfortable in our home. Over a recent week we

> *The first law of our being is that we are set in a delicate network of interdependence with our fellow human beings and with the rest of God's creation.*
>
> *Archbishop Desmond Tutu (1931–)*

had five different groups eat meals in our home. Hospitality is not always easy, yet I've learned from others that it is the best way to build community.

One of the groups was comprised of neighbors on our street. We have started to work together in an intentional way to share tools, a garden, and automobiles. Everything that we buy has an environmental cost—extracting materials, manufacturing, transporting, and marketing all require a tremendous amount of resources. The more items we buy, the bigger our homes, garden sheds, garages, and storage units need to be to house all the stuff. The bigger our homes, the more hours we have to work to afford the bigger lifestyle, and the more time it takes to organize, clean, and care for all the things in our lives. It's an ever spiraling cycle. One way to change directions is to get to know your neighbors and begin to share. If my neighbors and I share infrequently used items, then we lower our collective environmental footprint. No neighborhood need own more than one chainsaw, power saw, copy of a particular movie, or extension ladder. Scripture is explicit about the need to share: *"Do not refuse anyone who wants to borrow from you"* (Matt. 5:42).

My neighborhood now hosts weekly potlucks. And when Nancy needed sawhorses today, she put out an e-mail to the neighbors on the street. Literally within five minutes, we heard a knock at the door. There was Steve, with several folding sawhorses in hand. His family was leaving on vacation later that day and wanted to be sure we received the sawhorses before departing. Mission accomplished: no need to spend money and use resources acquiring a tool that we only use once every few years.

> The life I touch for good or ill will touch another life, and that in turn another, until who knows where the trembling stops or in what far place my touch will be felt.
>
> Frederick Buechner (1926–)

Indeed, all of us need to learn to borrow and lend gladly. For many, the church is the focal point of the community. Churches are natural places to give, borrow, and lend. Perhaps you can start a share board to post resources you are willing to lend or need to borrow. Or start a share board online. Since I used to be a carpenter, I have lent out many tools over the years, some of which were never returned, or returned in less than ideal shape. As a Christian, I know that these tools never really belonged to me—everything I "own" belongs to God. My advice is that we should all try to return borrowed items in as good or better condition, but we should expect items that we lend to not always come back in their original condition—a small price to pay for living life together.

Sharing is about generosity, and generosity is the engine of Christian community. Recently our state was hit with the worst ice storm ever recorded. When the ice melted, it looked as if a bomb had gone off. We had fallen trees and shattered limbs everywhere. Two of my neighbors spent an entire day cleaning up the aftermath in our yard. They asked for nothing. They would take nothing. "We just feel like helping you out because you're our neighbor," they said.

Communities often feel closest after they have been hit with a natural disaster. The loss of power, destruction of homes, and flooding forces us to share as a community; however, the biblical model is to share and work cooperatively *before* there is a natural disaster.

Sharing can start in the most minor and everyday manner. For instance, a number of our neighbors compost their vegetable matter in the bins we have in our backyard. We use that compost in our garden and share the produce. A friend of ours makes locally raised eggs available to a number of families, and Nancy organizes the purchase of beef from locally raised cows, which we share with neigh-

---

When a group of people are sailing in a boat, none of them has a right to bore a hole under his own seat.

Israel Meir ha-Kohen Kagan (1838–1933)

bors. All of these actions require some time, thought, and flexibility, but the result is that we all honor God's creation a little bit more each day by becoming better stewards of his blessings.

The modern-day advertisement for many chain restaurants features a large group or family eating and laughing together. Yet a chain restaurant is a poor substitute for hospitality offered by a family or neighborhood.

Just as important as celebrating together is working together. Nothing builds a sense of community like shared work. A survey of intentional communities throughout the ages will show shared work as the undergirding of a sense of belonging.

The small town we live in is, frankly, not particularly good looking. So a group of friends are getting together this spring to plant trees. Tree-lined streets are good for the community in many ways: they raise property values, reduce air-conditioning bills, and improve air quality. Trees invite birds and other wildlife, and, as any young child knows, they are fun to climb.

Many of us simply make plans to move if we are not satisfied with our sense of community or surroundings. However, the more biblical approach would be to seek the peace and prosperity of the place in which we dwell. We pay an enormous psychological cost for never being committed to a place. Perhaps one of the reasons so many of our communities have had little attention paid to aesthetics is our underlying philosophy that, like so many things in our lives, the land and neighborhoods around us are disposable. If we are unsatisfied, we can "purchase" a new community. How different this philosophy is from the sense of place we find throughout Scripture.

Keep in mind that our community is not composed of those who are already saints, but of those who are trying to become saints. Therefore let us be extremely patient with each other's faults and failures.

Mother Teresa (1910–1997)

In the Old Testament, cities were to have a buffer of nature around them; today's cities are surrounded by asphalt beltways. We are more likely to be committed to the principles of good stewardship if we think we are going to be around for a while. For instance, renters, by and large, do not take care of a property as well as owners. Similarly, transient people for the most part are less likely to commit to land-stewardship projects that unfold over generations.

In the past, a church symbolized an anchor in time and place. Births, baptisms, marriages, deaths, and burials were centered on the church. Gravestones reminded us of the cycle of life, death, and hope.

Compare these churches with our modern sanctuaries. Rarely does a modern church have a graveyard beside it. Moreover, our new sanctuaries often are too large for intimate funerals and marriages. Is it any wonder that people seek "virtual communities" when there are so few real ones?

Sharing, lending, committing, and hospitality involve hard work. Making and serving a meal is more difficult than going to a restaurant. Yet, the rewards of fellowship are worth the price. On the very last night of his life, Christ got together with his disciples and shared a meal. Every time we meet with neighbors, friends, and strangers and break bread together, we reenact this most sacred of occasions.

One encouraging sign of change is the new monastic movement. This model of community is centered on the commitment by church members to be involved in one another's everyday lives, as well as the lives of their (often poor and urban) neighbors. I've been blessed by friendships with several of these new monastic groups, including the Vineyard Central Community in Cincinnati, Ohio, and Communality in Lexington, Kentucky.

Even if you are old, you must plant. Just as you found trees planted by others, you must plant them for your children.

Midrash Tanchuma, Kodashim 8,
Midrash Teachers (4th to 5th centuries)

In addition to new monastic communities, home churches are springing up throughout the country. I believe that these home churches are a vital way of fulfilling our longing for community life. In a similar way within megachurches, small groups act as communities within communities, providing a way to belong, to worship, and to share in the context of an often impersonal world.

Bonhoeffer—the brilliant German theologian who died a martyr in a Nazi concentration camp—talks about the grace that God affords us by allowing us to live in community with fellow believers. Bonhoeffer suggests that one of greatest blessings one can have is life together. As the first-century church found, life together is not always easy. Paul disagreed with Peter. When you reach out to your neighbors and build community, there will be friction. Sometimes there will be controversy. We have all been raised in an environment of hyperindividuality and must actively practice the skills that will allow us to live together in closer community. We must pray for God's grace. We must practice tolerance and act as if tolerance were a verb.

You may have heard the saying "If you look for the perfect church and find one, it will no longer be perfect once you join." The same is probably true for neighborhoods. The model of the large suburban home situated in the middle of an acre or two of grass connected to its neighbor by driveways and pavement is not only bad for the earth, it is probably not healthy for those who live there.

No one knows for sure what heaven looks like, although many have tried to imagine. In all the musings about the city of God, heaven is never described as a place with duplicates of lawn mowers, recreational equipment, and two cars in every garage. In truth, it probably more closely resembles the communities described in the

> We have all known the long loneliness and we have learned that the only solution is love and that love comes with community.
>
> *Dorothy Day (1897–1980)*

book of Acts, and the Bruderhof community I visited in the Catskills of New York.

Everyone wants to live in a great community—but the definition of *great* can vary, depending on who you ask. In *The Great Divorce*, C. S. Lewis depicts neighborhoods in hell with houses separated by acres of land. Napoleon lives in the middle of a vast estate, where all the houses keep moving away from each other.

By contrast, both the Old Testament and the New Testament describe God's people living in close proximity. Perhaps it's time for all of us to start creating the City of God by reaching out to others in our own communities, no matter where we reside. Through the small acts of sharing tools, starting community gardens, carpooling, tree lining streets, running errands for one another, and extending a helping hand, we will all use fewer resources and demonstrate greater respect for God's creation.

A community needs a soul if it is to become a true home for human beings. You, the people, must give it this soul.

Pope John Paul II (1920–2005)

Tending the Garden
What you can do to encourage community

- Memorize one or more Bible verses about community, such as Philippians 2:3–4.

- Pick up trash in the neighborhood when you go on walks.

- Form an ecoteam of environmentally concerned friends and neighbors.

- Shop at a farmers' market and get to know the people who grow your food.

- Make a greater effort to carpool and coordinate errands with neighbors.

- Coordinate meals for someone in the neighborhood going through a difficult time.

- Beautify your neighborhood through gardens and tree planting.

- Coordinate a neighborhood block party or potluck dinner.

- Volunteer regularly for a community organization.

- Spend time daily talking to neighbors.

- Pray for the people on your street.

- Share produce from your garden, extra baked goods, or soup with a neighbor.

- Shop at a local business instead of a chain store.

- Perform an act of kindness for someone in the neighborhood, like offering to babysit so the parents can have a night out, or shoveling a sidewalk.

- Invite a young or elderly couple over for dinner.

- Lend and borrow rather than buying new.

- Advertise and give away unwanted items on www.craigslist.org or www.freecycle.org.

- Attend a local school play, art show, or concert in the park.

- Talk to local officials to find out what your town is doing to protect the environment and how you can help.

- Learn more about relational tithing through www.relationaltithe.com and Christian medical noninsurance at www.medi-share.org.

- Greet new families within a week of their arrival in the neighborhood.

- Talk to neighbors about purchasing expensive, infrequently used items together.

Adapted with permission from Go Green, Save Green: A Simple Guide to Saving Time, Money and God's Green Earth *(Nancy Sleeth, Tyndale, 2009). For more ideas, visit www.blessedearth.org.*

ELEVEN

Simplicity and Consumerism
Philippians

Rejoice in the Lord always; again I will say, Rejoice. Let
your gentleness be known to everyone. The Lord is near. Do
not worry about anything, but in everything by prayer and
supplication with thanksgiving let your requests be made
known to God. And the peace of God, which surpasses all
understanding, will guard your hearts and your minds in Christ
Jesus. Finally, beloved, whatever is true, whatever is honorable,
whatever is just, whatever is pure, whatever is pleasing,
whatever is commendable, if there is any excellence and if there
is anything worthy of praise, think about these things. Keep on
doing the things that you have learned and received and heard
and seen in me, and the God of peace will be with you.

(Phil. 4:4–9)

At home I write at an old desk pulled off the dump at the Navel
Ordinance Lab in White Oak, Maryland, in 1960. It is a standard
government-issue, quarter-sawn oak model dating back to the for-
ties. The desk has file drawers on either side of a large center drawer.
The working surface is three feet by five feet so I can get a multitude
of papers and books on it. Above the top drawers on both sides, the
desk has pull-out writing surfaces, on which my childhood friends
once etched their initials. The desk was discarded along with other
oak desks and file cabinets so that new grey metal ones could take

their place; these in turn have probably been cast off for laminated plastic ones. That's progress.

Our lives may be largely defined by what we keep and what we discard. Christ was abandoned on the cross, despised and rejected. Yet just because something is thrown away doesn't mean that it wasn't worth saving.

Today we live in a time of hyperconsumerism and high turnover. We move every half dozen years or so. We get rid of desks, countertops, and phones even though they are still serviceable. We discard spouses and families that were once the apple of our eye.

The Bible, however, calls for us to live a very different kind of life, one governed by simplicity and humility. Simplicity as a way of life brings us closer to God. It is a means of receiving God's grace as he transforms us. Simplicity helps us disconnect from the worldly concerns that destroy God's creation and, instead, engage in redemptive actions that heal.

The opposite of simplicity is blind consumerism. A consumerist way of life tells us we never have enough. Formica countertops are out; granite is in. Wide ties are dated; skinny ties are hip. Our kitchens need makeovers, as do our bodies, wardrobes, and marriages. If simplicity brings us closer to God, consumerism draws us to the devil.

I once had a patient come into the ER for a complaint I've long since forgotten, but I have not forgotten the man. He was a quiet sort of gentleman who lived alone and worked a solitary job. I asked about his passions and interests. Music—he loved music. I also love music. One afternoon, the patient invited me to his small apartment, which was lined with old-fashioned records. When he played

---

The primary requirement for the change is a longing to be transformed by God.

"As a deer longs for flowing streams, so longs my soul for you, O God. My soul thirsts for God, for the living God. When shall I come and behold the face of God?" (Ps. 42:1–2).

a favorite recording, he was nearly moved to tears. He sat transfixed through the entire side, using a record player that probably cost no more than a hundred dollars. His record collection was modest but beloved. At the time, no one any longer manufactured "vinyl." (Ironically, record manufacture has come back, and the average pressing costs twice what a CD does.) Occasionally he picked up a used recording at a yard sale for less than a dollar.

I met another gentleman a few weeks later. When asked, he also said that music was his hobby. "Would you like to come and hear my new system?" he asked. I made time to drop by. This fellow was of far greater means than the first gentleman. His system cost what one would pay for an average car. He popped one CD in after another— never waiting until a song was finished before going to the next. I could not picture him moved to tears or excited enough to play air guitar. I asked how many records he owned. "About three thousand records, and closer to seven thousand CDs," he replied. I couldn't help but do the math. At forty hours a week, it would take nearly five years to listen to everything just once. He had the largest collection I've ever seen, yet he'd lost the love of music.

How much to take in, what to keep, and what to get rid of? Simplicity doesn't just have to do with food, clothing, handbags, and cars; it's about what we put into our minds, what we listen to, and where we spend our time. Editing what we put into our hearts and our lives leads us along a less consumeristic path—one that heals creation rather than harms it.

Over my salvaged oak desk I have four small pieces of paper taped to a bookcase. One is a slip of paper with a bit of advice written by a jailed political prisoner two thousand years ago. It is about what to keep, and what to cast away: *"Beloved, whatever is true, whatever*

> **All of us are slaves to sin. We are all**
>
> *"under the power of sin, as it is written: 'There is no one who is righteous, not even one'"* (Rom. 3:9–10).

is honorable, whatever is just, whatever is pure, whatever is pleasing, whatever is commendable, if there is any excellence and if there is anything worthy of praise, think about these things" (Phil. 4:8).

When Paul wrote this advice in a letter to the Christians in Macedonia, he was in chains. Paul was a former high-ranking Jewish Pharisee who gave up everything to become a follower of Christ. Over the years, Paul suffered some tremendous hardships. The next time you're having a difficult day, consider this partial list of ordeals Paul underwent in his ministry:

> Five times I have received from the Jews the forty lashes minus one. Three times I was beaten with rods. Once I received a stoning. Three times I was shipwrecked; for a night and a day I was adrift at sea; on frequent journeys, in danger from rivers, danger from bandits, danger from my own people, danger from Gentiles, danger in the city, danger in the wilderness, danger at sea, danger from false brothers and sisters; in toil and hardship, through many a sleepless night, hungry and thirsty, often without food, cold and naked. *(2 Cor. 11:24–27)*

Paul has been dipped, dunked, stoned, and spat upon; now in chains, facing death, he worries about his jailers. In this most simple and humble state, he writes his friends in the east and urges them to set their minds toward "anything worthy of praise." For us today, as for Paul, a multitude of distractions can draw our thoughts away from God and caring for his creation.

Nearly every person on the planet thinks he or she is a kind person and a good steward. The question is, how do we get from

---

Although we may wish to live less worldly lives, such transformation is impossible on our own.

"If with Christ you died to the elemental spirits of the universe, why do you live as if you still belonged to the world?" (Col. 2:20).

thinking we are thoughtful caretakers to being like Paul, Mother Teresa, or Dietrich Bonhoeffer? We can pray—nothing works without prayer—but most of us are going to have to work at it as well. You may have heard the saying that if you pray for food, you should have a shovel in one hand and seeds in the other. Subtracting consumerism and waste from our lives requires work.

Many Christians are familiar with voluntarily giving up a certain worldly vice for Lent, the forty days leading up to Easter. Some stop eating candy, while others forego caffeine or alcohol. The purpose of the exercise is to give up a minor vice to both celebrate Christ's victory over sin and to share a tiny part of Christ's suffering. The point is not to show others what a great Christian you are, but to be able to understand the sacrifice of Christ. It is a time for becoming less attached to worldly things, and more focused on God.

Acts of sacrifice and simplicity such as abstaining during Lent were nearly universal in the Christian world until the Reformation; they have been slowly making their way back into the Protestant denominations. The book of Acts records numerous examples of Christ and members of the early church participating in periods of prayer and fasting. A few decades ago, one of the most common vices to give up for Lent was smoking. Many hoped that after forty days without a smoke, they would be delivered from the habit for good. Some didn't make it a day, some cheated, others made it and then relapsed, and others were delivered from the need to smoke forever.

What is seen as a blessing to one generation can be viewed differently by another. Tobacco was once considered an adjunct to social well-being. It was the engine of the Revolutionary War economy. But

---

A desire for simplicity opens the door for God to change us. This transformation is a free gift that only Jesus can offer; however, first we must understand how

"the abundance of grace and the free gift of righteousness exercise dominion in life through the one man, Jesus Christ" (Rom. 5:17).

few today argue that tobacco is good for anyone. Tobacco is addictive and works by changing our brain chemistry. I wonder what Paul would advise about the accepted addictive behaviors of today, such as television, computers, and electronic gaming?

In Paul's day, people went to the city gate, temple, market, and coliseum to interact with others. What they encountered depended on the functions they attended. Today, we live in an electronic and increasingly virtual world. One need not walk to the temple to engage a pagan prostitute; we can find pornography on the computer or television. If we are bored and want to see someone killing another person, we don't need to go down to the coliseum and watch the gladiators duke it out. We can enjoy *The Texas Chainsaw Massacre* or *Kill Bill* from the comfort of our recliners. If we enjoy endless gossip and speculation, we can tune in to talk radio or *Entertainment Tonight.*

A twentieth-century prophet who predicted the immense impact that television would have on our society is E. B. White, author of the childhood classics *Stuart Little* and *Charlotte's Web* as well as Strunk and White's *Manual of Style,* and a longtime editor of the *New Yorker.* He put together a collection of essays between 1938 and 1944 titled *One Man's Meat,* which has remained in continual publication ever since. The book is on my top-twenty must-read list. When White saw a demonstration of the television in 1938, he made several prescient predictions:

> Clearly the race is between the loud speaking and the soft, between the chemist of RCA and the angel of God. Radio has already given sound a wide currency, and sound "effects" are taking the place once enjoyed by sound itself. Television will enormously enlarge the eye's range, and like radio, will adver-

---

We need to be quiet in order to hear God. *"Be still, and know that I am God!"* (Ps. 46:10).

tise the Elsewhere. Together with the tabs, the mags, and the movies, it will insist that we forget the primary and the near in favor of the secondary and the remote. More hours in every twenty-four will be spent digesting ideas, sounds, images— distant and concocted.

If White was rightly concerned about the potential impact of television, consider how appalled he—or Paul—would be by the content and consumption of programming today. For example, imagine Paul's reaction to a show that films people in prison, for the sake of entertaining viewers. I don't think this is what the Bible means when it says, *"Remember those who are in prison, as though you were in prison with them; those who are being tortured, as though you your-selves were being tortured"* (Heb. 13:3). In fact, reality shows like this are voyeuristic, the antithesis of the compassion and empathy called for by Scripture. What would Jesus say about a reality series featuring women who compete to sleep with a rock star?

Paul, rather, calls for us to be imitators of Christ:

Be imitators of God, therefore, as dearly loved children and live a life of love, just as Christ loved us and gave himself up for us as a fragrant offering and sacrifice to God. But among you there must not be even a hint of sexual immorality, or of any kind of impurity, or of greed, because these are improper for God's holy people. Nor should there be obscenity, foolish talk or coarse joking, which are out of place, but rather thanksgiving. For of this you can be sure: No immoral, impure or greedy person—such a man is an idolater—has any inheritance in the kingdom of Christ and of God. *(Eph. 5:1–5, NIV)*

And we need to be patient. *"For everything there is a season, and a time for every matter under heaven"* (Eccles. 3:1).

What Paul is advocating is a pure and simple life dedicated to godly concerns, not worldly ones. The Bible is pretty clear about what Jesus would make of entire networks devoted to food, home decorating, fashion, or sports. Christ's instructions tell us explicitly not to fill our minds with such concerns: *"Do not worry about your life, what you will eat or what you will drink, or about your body, what you will wear. Is not life more than food and the body more than clothing?"* (Matt. 6:25).

Not all media, of course, is bad. Several years ago, I took a group of teens to see the documentary *Winged Migration,* a visually stunning film about the migration of birds. All the young people seemed to enjoy it, but one had a question: "Is it real?" This high schooler had spent so much time in front of television and computer screens that he could no longer discern the difference between fact and fiction.

Yet most media, unlike documentaries like *Winged Migration* or *Planet Earth,* are not educational or inspirational. The majority of what we watch on the tube is escapist in nature. It kills time, while killing our souls. Christ, however, warned us not to let ourselves be caught "sleeping." He wasn't referring to actual sleeping at night, but to spending our time dazed—not focused on loving God and our neighbors. Intellectually, we know that our days could end at any moment, and yet we waste time as if our earthly life will go on forever. In America the average seventy-year-olds will have spent ten years of their waking lives passively watching television. The average child in America spends six and a half hours per day in front of a screen. That's the kind of sleeping Jesus is telling us to avoid.

> **Part of the journey is seeking which habits we should eliminate— what keeps us at arm's length from God.**
>
> *"Let us also lay aside every weight and the sin that clings so closely, and let us run with perseverance the race that is set before us"* (Heb. 12:1).

Adopting a simpler life can be boiled down to a simple question: what to edit, and what to keep? My family hasn't owned a television for about eight years, but occasionally I am confronted by one in a hotel room, and I'll turn it on. A scroll through a hundred channels is enough to get me anxious. Maybe my bathroom needs to be updated. I ought to lose weight, yet don't I deserve a break today? What about the invisible germs lurking in my house that I've never paid attention to before? Do I need a home alarm system? Should Nancy wash the grey streaks out of her hair, and should I do something about that thinning area on the top of my head?

My car has a few dents in it, and that stain on the carpet—is it time for a new one? I'm told I should be talking to my broker, and that some listen more than others—does this mean I have to get a broker? I feel a bit tired on the road; do I need a power drink, leaner cereal, or to ask my doctor about an antidepressant? Do I smell? Does my house need to be painted a new color? Would life be complete if I traveled to shake Mickey Mouse's gloved hand? If I check the news on the top of every hour, will I stay informed?

Paul's question: What is true and just? What is worthy of praise? What distracts me from a God-centered life? My advice, based upon Paul's wisdom, is that we need to edit out much of what the world is trying to sell us. The goal of all the ads for cars, skincare products, and clothing is to make us feel discontent and buy the concept that we would be happier if we only added Product X to our laundry, hair, skin, or lawn.

This bombardment of discontent is the opposite of Paul's message:

> **Just because we *can* do anything doesn't mean we *should*.**
>
> *"'All things are lawful for me,' but not all things are beneficial. 'All things are lawful for me,' but I will not be dominated by anything'"* (1 Cor. 6:12).

I know what it is to have little, and I know what it is to have plenty. In any and all circumstances I have learned the secret of being well-fed and of going hungry, of having plenty and of being in need. I can do all things through him who strengthens me. *(Phil. 4:12–13)*

Paul's continued call to the Philippians was to be joyful and content. His formula for getting there was to love God, love our neighbor, and be happy with what we have.

I'm glad my desk was pulled off the dump. It works fine. The earth is being dug up, cut down, and dismantled to meet the needs and cravings of a population that can only be satisfied with newer, better, and more. The way to cut back on the misuse of resources is to live more simply and be content with what we have. One way to accomplish this is to remove the nonstop assault of advertisements from our lives. America would be a better country if we pursued whatever is true, whatever is honorable, whatever is just, whatever is pure, whatever is pleasing, and whatever is commendable. We should edit out the vulgar, greed, and selfishness as much as possible, and add in what is excellent and worthy of praise.

The journey toward a simpler, less consumeristic life is not easy to take alone; we can be more successful if we work within a supportive community. If you cannot take one day a week for rest, begin with four hours. If getting rid of your television forever seems too daunting, unplug it for a month and keep a journal of how this change affects your thoughts, your activities, and your relationships. Try to

The other half of the journey is seeking which new habits will bring us closer to God.

"Whatever is true, whatever is honorable, whatever is just, whatever is pure, whatever is pleasing, whatever is commendable, if there is any excellence and if there is anything worthy of praise, think about these things" (Phil. 4:8).

make these changes with friends, church, and family. If you're the mom or dad, unplug your children from television for forty days. Take them outside and plant a tree like Abraham did. Read them Psalm 104, and then enjoy the simple pleasure of spending time in God's creation on a daily basis.

Simplicity is life enhancing. Disconnecting from consumerism and adopting a simpler lifestyle helps us edit out the destructive stuff and welcome in the redemptive. Simplicity allows us to be transformed by God's grace into people who take care of God's creation, rather than destroy it. It helps us do what we cannot do alone to save the planet.

The practice of simplicity demands that we alter life-as-usual. When you are feeling like life is out of control, ask yourself two questions: What am I currently *doing* that, if eliminated, would open me up more to God's work of grace in my life? And what am I *not doing* that would help me be a better steward of God's creation? Your honest answers will always lead you down the right path.

The practice of simple living will help us become better stewards of creation by helping us resist actions that destroy and embrace those that redeem.

"God did not give us a spirit of cowardice but rather a spirit of power and of love and of self-discipline" (2 Tim. 1:7).

Tending the Garden
What you can do to combat consumerism

- Take a one-month television fast. Keep a journal. Record what has changed about your relationship with friends, family, and God.

- Replace half an hour of computer gaming with a walk around the block.

- Turn off the radio in the car, and instead use the time to fellowship with God.

- Fast one meal each week and donate the money saved to a hunger-related cause.

- Start a vegetable garden. Pray while you work the earth.

- Hang clothes on the line. Pay attention to the sounds, sights, and smells of nature while you are outside.

- Select a cue—the computer chime when e-mail is received, a glance at the clock, a discrete beep from your watch—to remind yourself to say a short prayer. Your meditation can be something as simple as "Be still, and know that I am God," or something longer, like a silent recitation of the Lord's Prayer.

- Get in the habit of saying a prayer of thanks not only at meals, but when you fill up the car with gas, when you turn on the water to brush your teeth, and when you adjust the thermostat. Cultivate an attitude of gratitude.

- Give up an addiction for forty days. Pray for intercession by the Holy Spirit and God's strength. Your period of abstinence can involve something physical—cigarettes, alcohol, chocolate, desserts. Or it can involve a habit—criticism of a particular person, interrupting when someone is speaking, leaving lights and computers on when you leave a room.

- Go on a long walk in nature by yourself. Make walking part of your Sabbath practice.

- Confess to God and to a supportive friend a behavior that harms creation. Ask for God's help to change the behavior, and ask your friend to hold you accountable.

- Go on a media fast for a week—no newspaper, no radio, no television, no Internet surfing. At the end of the week, reflect on any changes. Do you experience symptoms of withdrawal at first? Do you feel less anxious at the end of the week? Was there anything of eternal value that you missed while unplugged?

- If you do not read from the Bible every day already, try doing so for one month. Start with ten minutes. Do it at the same time every day—before work, on your lunch break, or when you get into bed at night.

- Spend fifteen minutes outside every day for one week, just looking at God's creation and thanking him for all his sustaining gifts. Or hang a bird feeder by your window, and watch the birds.

- Try to find godly things to do or say for which you will not be thanked.

Adapted with permission from Go Green, Save Green: A Simple Guide to Saving Time, Money and God's Green Earth *(Nancy Sleeth, Tyndale, 2009). For more ideas, visit www.blessedearth.org.*

TWELVE

Sacrifice
Colossians

He has rescued us from the power of darkness and transferred us into the kingdom of his beloved Son, in whom we have redemption, the forgiveness of sins. He is the image of the invisible God, the firstborn of all creation; for in him all things in heaven and on earth were created, things visible and invisible, whether thrones or dominions or rulers or powers—all things have been created through him and for him. He himself is before all things, and in him all things hold together. He is the head of the body, the church; he is the beginning, the firstborn from the dead, so that he might come to have first place in everything. For in him all the fullness of God was pleased to dwell, and through him God was pleased to reconcile to himself all things, whether on earth or in heaven, by making peace through the blood of his cross.

And you who were once estranged and hostile in mind, doing evil deeds, he has now reconciled in his fleshly body through death, so as to present you holy and blameless and irreproachable before him—provided that you continue securely established and steadfast in the faith, without shifting from the hope promised by the gospel that you heard, which has been proclaimed to every creature under heaven. *(Col. 1:13–23)*

Last year I was asked to give a commencement address. Of all the graduation speeches I have heard over the years, I can only remember one—the speech given at Nancy's college graduation, thirty years ago.

I remembered the speech for its simple message, not *how* it was said. In fact, I do not think there has ever been a more disjointed, rambling, nonlinear commencement speech. At the time I thought that the little old lady addressing the crowd was bonkers. Although many in the audience stared at the podium in awe, quite a few around us thought she was out of touch with reality, as reflected in the criticisms they spoke out loud.

So when I was asked to give the commencement address at a seminary, I contacted Nancy's alma mater, and they kindly sent me a transcript of that speech. My recollection was not wrong. The organization and word choice of the address left much to be desired. But the message was, and is, the most beautiful I have ever heard. What the speaker said can be summed up in two sentences:

Love God, and give your life in service to others.
Nothing else matters.

At the time, the author of this message was called Mother Teresa, but it is a safe bet that someday she will be called St. Teresa.

Today, almost everyone alive knows about Mother Teresa and her work with the poor in India. She founded the Missionaries of Charity, a group of women working among the world's forgotten and destitute people. In an age when other orders lack volunteers, the

God sacrificed his only Son to reconcile all of creation.

"In him all the fullness of God was pleased to dwell, and through him God was pleased to reconcile to himself all things, whether on earth or in heaven, by making peace through the blood of his cross" *(Col. 1:19–20).*

Missionaries of Charity still have women queuing up to serve. Why? It probably has something to do with a truth that Gandhi, the president of her adopted country, espoused in his Seven Deadly Social Sins: "Religion without sacrifice is a sin."

Mother Teresa's own writings reveal that for decades she struggled with her faith. She had doubts, yet she persisted in a life of sacrifice and poverty to the end. She worked tirelessly for a God she sometimes was not even sure existed. Was she a fool? Should any of us give up things now for a future we have never seen?

Living without comfort, security, or safety is called poverty. Forgoing these blessings when one can obtain them is called sacrifice.

We are a generation that does not care for words like *discipline, denial, sin, restraint, obedience,* or *sacrifice.* This aversion impacts our reluctance to make any changes that are inconvenient—from removing lead in gasoline to placing a deposit on bottles. Why should anyone tell us what to do? Churchgoers or not, we serve iGod, and iGod demands nothing. We get to choose what color and add-on features our iGods have. They can be worshipped in traditional, contemporary, or cable modes—you can have it your way.

The most common reason that people object to living more humble, meek, and less consumerist lives is not that they believe their world will come to an end if they don't. It is not that they are not worried about the next generation. Rather, they fear they will be asked to sacrifice.

A few years ago, I attended a conference where a church leader advised me never to mention the word *sacrifice.* "Talk about that, and you'll lose everybody. Appeal to their common sense," was the

His sacrifice makes us agents of reconciliation for all of creation.

"If anyone is in Christ, there is a new creation: everything old has passed away; see, everything has become new! All this is from God, who reconciled us to himself through Christ, and has given us the ministry of reconciliation" (2 Cor. 5:17–18).

cleric's advice. "Self-interest is the only thing that motivates people to change." But did Mother Teresa live with lepers in the slums because it made sense, or helped her get ahead?

People of faith bring many things to the environmental movement, including music, community, hospitality, love of the Creator, and the Sabbath rest. However, the most remarkable attribute that Jesus brings to the table doesn't make sense at all. It is not about having your best life now, or buying anything that you can afford, or purchasing things that you can't afford on credit. The illogical marvel that Jesus introduced to the world is sacrifice. From his first night in a stable to his last hours on the cross, Jesus was all about sacrifice. His life was a sacrifice. As a wise pastor once said, "If you don't believe in sacrifice, you might as well quit church and meet on Wednesdays for lunch like every other well-intentioned social group. It will cost less, and you'll get better food."

The message of Jesus is about helping *your neighbor* have his best life now. In a time of the prosperity gospel, such a message is at best inconvenient and at worst rejected. People with vested interests, in ancient times and today, seldom want to give them up. What about clean air and water? Are we accepting the truth that each day clean air and water become scarcer? Are we each living sacrificially to protect the water, land, and skies that were created by God to sustain every generation? Everyone believes that ark building is a great idea once it has begun to rain. The trick is beginning an ark six months before the flood.

> **Christ's ultimate sacrifice on the cross encourages and empowers us to give up our selfish desires.**
>
> *"The love of Christ urges us on, because we are convinced that one has died for all; therefore all have died. And he died for all, so that those who live might live no longer for themselves, but for him who died and was raised for them" (2 Cor. 5:14–15).*

We can begin building our metaphorical ark by accepting God's truth and living sacrificially. "All truth is God's truth," so the saying goes. Yet as the truth, the light, and the way, Jesus is denied repeatedly. During his life Jesus found acceptance from a motley crew, including the odd sailor, the IRS agent, and the woman at a well; however, for everyone who brought Jesus a drink, a dozen others wanted to stone him or throw him off a cliff. Jesus wasn't elevator music; he was more like rap or country. You either loved him or you reviled him. Few can be lukewarm about a message that calls for personal sacrifice.

I find it interesting that no one who chronicled the life of Jesus described what he looked like. But we can find a prophetic description of him in Isaiah:

For he shall grow up before him as a tender plant, and as a root out of a dry ground: he hath no form nor comeliness; and when we shall see him, there is no beauty that we should desire him. He is despised and rejected of men; a man of sorrows, and acquainted with grief: and we hid as it were our faces from him; he was despised, and we esteemed him not.

Surely he hath borne our griefs, and carried our sorrows: yet we did esteem him stricken, smitten of God, and afflicted.

Instead of seeking worldly interests, we are to serve the interests of others.

"Let each of you look not to your own interests, but to the interests of others. Let the same mind be in you that was in Christ Jesus, who, though he was in the form of God, did not regard equality with God as something to be exploited, but emptied himself, taking the form of a slave, being born in human likeness. And being found in human form, he humbled himself and became obedient to the point of death—even death on a cross" (Phil. 2:4–8).

But he was wounded for our transgressions, he was bruised for our iniquities: the chastisement of our peace was upon him; and with his stripes we are healed. All we like sheep have gone astray; we have turned every one to his own way; and the LORD hath laid on him the iniquity of us all. *(Isa. 53:2–6, KJV)*

Many may recognize a few stanzas from Handel's magnificent choral work *Messiah* in these passages. Jesus is not described as especially handsome. Rather, he is compared to a plant. If central casting carefully read these verses from Isaiah, a thirty-year-old Danny DeVito might get the role of Jesus.

He grew up like a root . . . like a tender plant . . . and like a plant he had no beauty that would attract us to him. The language Isaiah uses to predict the coming of the Messiah reflects our propensity to overlook plants that seem to have "no beauty." Humanity rejects Jesus, just as it rejects much of nature. Indeed, the Bible says that all of creation *groans* because of mankind's sin (Rom. 8:22). John 3:16 states that God sent his only Son to straighten things out.

The sacrifice that God asks of us is to act justly and live humbly.

"Listen to what the LORD says: 'Stand up, plead your case before the mountains; let the hills hear what you have to say. Hear, O mountains, the LORD's accusation; listen, you everlasting foundations of the earth. For the LORD has a case against his people; he is lodging a charge against Israel. My people, what have I done to you? How have I burdened you? Answer me. I brought you up out of Egypt and redeemed you from the land of slavery. I sent Moses to lead you, also Aaron and Miriam.'. . . Will the LORD be pleased with thousands of rams, with ten thousand rivers of oil? Shall I offer my firstborn for my transgression, the fruit of my body for the sin of my soul? He has showed you, O man, what is good. And what does the LORD require of you? To act justly and to love mercy and to walk humbly with your God" (Mic. 6:1–4, 7–8, NIV).

Part of restoration involves a right relationship with nature. Even a cursory examination of the life of Christ, as well as his scriptural names, points to a green Jesus who acts sacrificially. The *"firstborn of all creation"* (Col. 1:15) begins as a baby in a manger surrounded and warmed by animals. The *"chief shepherd"* (1 Pet. 5:4) is visited by sheep herders at birth and spends his first forty days of ministry on a wilderness camping trip. Jesus calls four fishermen to become his disciples. Next, he ascends a mountainside and promises that the meek will inherit the earth. He states that heaven is God's throne and the earth is God's footstool. The fish obey him in a miraculous catch. The *"good shepherd"* picks wheat, talks about the fruit of life, describes the four soils, tells of growing seeds, and preaches about weeds, yeast, mustard seeds, and pearls—the only gem made from a living organism.

If that is not enough "earthy" ministry, the *"bread of life"* (John 6:35) calms a storm, walks on water, turns a couple of fish and a few slices of bread into a feast for thousands, gets his taxes from a fish's mouth, talks about God's caring for flowers and birds, teaches about lost sheep, longs to protect Jerusalem like a mother hen, and tells parables about vineyard workers.

As the *"Lion of the tribe of Judah"* (Rev. 5:5), Jesus enters Jerusalem on the back of a previously unridden colt while the crowd waves palm fronds in the animal's face. Those of us who grew up on farms know that it is not possible to calmly ride an unbroken colt

---

When we fail to live humbly, the earth pays the price.

"The earth is defiled by its people; they have disobeyed the laws, violated the statutes and broken the everlasting covenant. Therefore a curse consumes the earth; its people must bear their guilt" (Isa. 24:5–6, NIV). *"Your own conduct and actions have brought this upon you. This is your punishment. How bitter it is! How it pierces to the heart!. . . Disaster follows disaster; the whole land lies in ruins"* (Jer. 4:18, 20, NIV).

surrounded by loud crowds throwing branches in the path. Riding a colt that has never been ridden is called bronco busting, and it can't be done sidesaddle. Yet God uses this miracle and many others to reveal his will through nature.

Christ's connection with God's creation continues to the end of his short life. The *"morning star"* (Rev. 22:16) washes the earth off his disciples' feet. Throughout his ministry, the *"Root of David"* (Rev. 5:5) repeatedly retreats to nature to be alone with his Father. On his last night he agonizes in a garden. In the end, he stretches out his callused carpenter's hands and dies on a cross that was once a tree. Three days later Mary comes to visit the tomb of the *"Author of life"* (Acts 3:15). It is empty. She turns and sees a gardener, and yet it is not just any gardener; it is the risen Jesus Christ. He is *"the last Adam"* (1 Cor. 15:45) sent to protect and tend the garden, God's green earth. The gardener that Mary sees is not a mere fancy or mistake of Scripture. He is the new Adam, the triumphal resurrection. When Rembrandt paints this moment, Christ is wearing the wide brim hat of the gardener while carrying a spade in his right hand (*The Resurrected Lord Appears to Mary Magdalene*, Royal Collection, Buckingham Palace).

Nearly a decade ago, when I first read through the entire Bible with a green lens, I was particularly struck by the comparison of the Messiah to a tender root and the prophecies that Jesus would die on a

> **If each of us can simply sacrifice our pride, then God will heal the land.**
>
> *"When I shut up the heavens so that there is no rain . . . if my people, who are called by my name, will humble themselves and pray and seek my face and turn from their wicked ways, then will I hear from heaven and will forgive their sin and will heal their land"* (2 Chron. 7:13–14, NIV).

tree. The connection between God, Jesus, and trees is not subtle, yet it could easily be lost on a generation that has never had the pleasure of climbing up a tree. Jesus found more than one of his followers in the company of a tree, including Nathanael, who initially dismissed Jesus because Jesus lived in Nazareth. *"Can anything good come out of Nazareth?"* (John 1:46), Nathanael asked. When Christ reveals that he not only saw Nathanael sitting under a fig tree, but heard his thoughts, Nathanael's skepticism is banished: "I saw you under the fig tree before Phillip called you" (John 1:48). In the shade of a tree, the Lord is present and hears our silent thoughts.

Later in his ministry, when Christ entered Jericho, a wealthy tax collector climbed a sycamore tree to get a better view of Jesus and his entourage. Christ ignores the crowd and looks up into the tree to find Zacchaeus. Jesus calls the man by name, and Zacchaeus shimmies down the tree and takes Jesus to his home for supper. Zacchaeus's response to Christ is a declaration that he will give half of everything he owns to the poor and refund four times what he has overcharged anyone on taxes.

It is not by chance that Christ says, "I am the true vine, and my father is the gardener" (John 15:1, NLT). In all, the Gospels record Jesus talking about fruit on over forty occasions. Believers are a "spiritual harvest," and those who spread the word about Christ are referred to as planters.

One of those planters was Martin Luther, the father of Protestantism, who speaks frequently of God's kingdom in terms of trees: "For in the true nature of things, if we rightly consider, every green tree is far more glorious than if it were made of gold and silver." Like

---

He assumed a body to bring help to suffering creatures. . . . He was both sacrifice and celebrant, sacrificial priest and God himself. He offered blood to God to cleanse the entire world.
    Quoted in Andrew Linzey, Compassion for Animals: Readings and Prayers, *St. Gregory Nazianzus (330–c. 389)*

so many of our ancestors, he shows hope for the future in the simple act of planting trees: "Even if I knew that tomorrow the world would go to pieces, I would still plant my apple tree." Planting trees is a sacrificial act. We plant trees not for ourselves, but for the enjoyment of future generations.

Clearly, going green requires sacrifice. Is Jesus, the ultimate sacrifice, green? If he is not, we have produced a tremendous amount of art and music about him that is wrong.

In my youth, I attended a church with no air-conditioning, no padded seats, and no short sermons. On hot days the windows were opened, and bumblebees would buzz around the hot sanctuary. Older women smelling of lavender water cooled themselves using fans made of printed paperboard. The fans resided in hymnbook racks on the backs of the pews. The fans had Bible verses or pictures printed on them and handles made from wood that resembled large Popsicle sticks. I recall one in particular, which had the following Bible passage:

The LORD is my shepherd; I shall not want.
He maketh me to lie down in green pastures:
he leadeth me beside the still waters.
He restoreth my soul:
he leadeth me in the paths of righteousness for his name's sake.
Yea, though I walk through the valley of the shadow of death,
I will fear no evil: for thou art with me;

> The seriousness of ecological degradation lays bare the depth of man's moral crisis. If an appreciation of the value of human life is lacking, we will also lose concern for others and for the earth itself. Simplicity, moderation and discipline, as well as the spirit of sacrifice, must become a part of everyday life.
> "Peace with God, Peace with Creation," World Day of Peace Message, Vatican City, January 1, 1990, Pope John Paul II (1920–2005)

thy rod and thy staff they comfort me.
Thou preparest a table before me in the presence of mine
    enemies:
thou anointest my head with oil;
my cup runneth over.
Surely goodness and mercy shall follow me all the days of my
    life:
and I will dwell in the house of the LORD for ever.
(Psalm 23:1–6, KJV)

On the other side of the fan was a picture. Jesus stood with a small lamb in one arm and a staff in his other hand. Surrounding him was the edge of the woods and a stream. Children followed Christ on his walk. It wasn't high art, but it was beautiful.

I'm not so sure that heaven doesn't in some way resemble the picture and verse on that fan. Lambs, green pastures, woods, streams, children, Jesus—it sounds like heaven to me. Jesus is about little children, about the next generation. We are to teach our children about Jesus, and pray for God's will to be done on earth as it is in heaven.

Throughout history artists have portrayed Jesus within the context of their culture. When the Dutch painted him, Jesus looks Dutch. When Caravaggio painted him, he looks Italian. I do not think it's wrong to paint Jesus as an African, Korean, or Northern

---

During the Divine Sacrifice, streams of Divine Grace flood into the world. Heaven and earth, Infinite and finite, Uncreated and created, God and man come together and become one, or rather, their already existing unity is realized.

The Eucharist, for an Orthodox Christian, is not so much a sudden intervention from above, as a gradual revelation of the divine presence which is always here.

The Church of the Eastern Christians, *Nicholas Zernov (1898–1980)*

European. We approach Christ through the lens of our times; biblical art reflects the people who make it.

Biblical art also reflects the landscapes and cityscapes of the times. For instance, Leonardo painted Renaissance Italy in the background of his religious art. The Limbourg brothers placed Holland in their magnificent religious miniatures. A survey of religious paintings now hanging in the Met, National Gallery, and Uffizi will show Middle Ages churches, Renaissance gardens, and nineteenth-century villas in the background as Christ and the saints go about their lives. The painters and the viewers cast Christ into their worlds.

Why, then, the nearly total lack of twenty-first-century paintings of Christ healing the poor at the edge of a blacktopped church parking lot, with hundreds of cars gleaming in the background? Why no Jesus on the turnpike, or at the strip mall, or large box store? Contrast our flimsy, short-sighted, maximum-square-footage-for-the-dollar world with cathedrals built to last for centuries. Is it possible that we are building a world so unlike what God intended that Jesus can no longer be pictured in it? Does our art reflect the current unwillingness to sacrifice for God the Creator and God's creation?

In a world of iGod, we seem to either love the Creator but disregard his creation, or love creation but forget about the Creator. We can sing praise songs to a God of wonder beyond our galaxy and

> *Reverence for life . . . does not allow the scholar to live for his science alone, even if he is very useful to the community in so doing. It does not permit the artist to exist only for his art, even if he gives inspiration to many by its means. It refuses to let the businessman imagine that he fulfills all legitimate demands in the course of his business activities. It demands from all that they should sacrifice a portion of their own lives for others.*
> "Ehrfurcht vor dem Leben," in The World of Albert Schweitzer, Albert Schweitzer (1875–1965)

toss trash out the window of our cars, or we can celebrate Earth Day while believing God is merely a crutch for the weak.

How, in God's name, have we become so estranged from the *"firstborn of all creation"* so beautifully celebrated in our doxology?

Praise God, from Whom all blessings flow;
Praise Him, all creatures here below;
Praise Him above, ye Heavenly Host;
Praise Father, Son, and Holy Ghost. Amen.

This doxology (Greek for *glory words*) is sung today in all manner of churches. It says that we sing praises to God along with all the creatures of the earth. Yet do we?

Giving praise to God is not only singing to him, but doing his bidding, even if it calls for sacrifice. The Old Testament is replete with laws regarding care of animals, fields, rivers, and all of creation. When Jesus comes on the scene, he ups the ante. We are to go even further than the letter of the law; we are to honor the intent of the law. For example, it is not enough to refrain from killing one's neighbor; we are not even to be angry, or say bad words about them (see Matthew 5). Similarly, not only are we forbidden from committing adultery; we must not even lust with our eyes. What, then, are the implications of the hundreds of laws that apply to the earth? If before the coming of Christ we were required to give animals one

---

The words and decrees of God become the law of nature. Therefore the decree which God uttered as a result of the disobedience of the first Adam, the decree of death and corruption, became a law of nature eternal and unchanging. For the abolition of this decree, the Son of God, our Lord Jesus Christ, was crucified and died, offering Himself as a sacrifice for the redemption of man from death.

The Sin of Adam, *"The Fall of Adam and the Decrees of God,"* Homily 38.3–4, St. Symeon the New Theologian (949–1022)

day in seven to rest, what is the intent of such laws for people "made perfect in Christ"?

If we are to be made perfect in Christ, then we need to be willing to sacrifice, like Christ. We need to change the way we live for the sake of preserving his creation. We need to do things that are inconvenient to help our global neighbors. And we need to invest in new infrastructure to leave clean air and pure water for future generations of God's humanity and all of his creatures.

Think of the earth as a ship. It is the only earth we have. If we destroy it, we have nowhere else to go. If the ship is sinking, as ours most assuredly is, we must make difficult choices to save it. Choices that involve sacrifice.

One famous ship, the USS *Dorchester*, was torpedoed on February 3, 1943. Many people on the ship perished instantly, yet four chaplains calmed the hundreds of survivors and helped them into lifeboats. In the end, four sailors waited without life vests of their own. The chaplains took off their own vests and handed them over to the sailors. That's Christianity, built on the model of Christ's sacrifice.

The future will hold in esteem those who are willing to sacrifice. The earth is the life vest of all humanity. We have no spare livable planet at hand. We need to stop grabbing for all we can get and start living simpler, humbler, meeker lives. In order to do that, we will need help. We need to pray for strength.

As Mother Teresa said in the graduation speech I heard thirty years ago, "We need to find God, and God cannot be found in noise and restlessness. God is the friend of silence. See how nature—trees and flowers and grass—grow in silence. See the stars, the moon, and the sun, how they move in silence. The more we receive in silent prayer, the more we can give in our active life."

It is time for us to start giving back sacrificially to God's creation, rather than destroying it.

Tending the Garden
What you can do sacrificially to care for creation

Many of the practical tips listed in the preceding chapters may be inconvenient, but they do not involve any major sacrifices. This list ups the ante a bit, calling for changes that are sacrificial— involving a commitment of time or money. Pick a few that you can perform in gladness, in light of the ultimate sacrifice of Christ on the cross. These twenty suggestions for long-term investments you can make today to prepare for the future are listed in approximate order of cost, from low to high:

- Green power from your public utility
- Composting system
- Clothesline
- Replacing all lightbulbs
- Dual-flush toilet
- Organic food
- Thermal curtains
- Solar lawn mower
- Rain garden, native landscaping
- Efficient home electronics—laptops instead of desktops, Energy Star printers, televisions, DVD players
- Electric bike or moped
- Energy-saving appliances—dishwasher, refrigerator, front-load washer, efficient dryer with moisture sensor
- Insulation in the attic, exterior walls, basement, and crawl spaces
- Gray water system

- High-efficiency furnace, air conditioner, or heat pump
- Solar water heater
- Double-pane windows with low-e (low-emissivity) coatings
- Geothermal heating and cooling
- Hybrid car
- Solar panels

What's the best way to be prepared for energy shortages? Move to a smaller, Energy Star home (townhouses and condos are most efficient) within walking or biking distance of work, school, and shopping.

Adapted with permission from Go Green, Save Green: A Simple Guide to Saving Time, Money and God's Green Earth *(Nancy Sleeth, Tyndale, 2009). For more ideas, visit www.blessedearth.org.*

Acknowledgments

I wish to thank Mickey Maudlin, Marlene Baer, Alison Petersen, and the rest of the team at HarperOne for suggesting this book and making it happen. Greg Daniel—you are more than the best literary agent in the lower forty-eight; you are a great person. David Wenzel, Santino Stoner, Corey Petrick—I love you guys. Thanks for making movie magic. Will Sears—I am grateful for your faith, work, and dedication. Sandy VanderZicht—thanks for being one of the very first to believe. Same goes to Diane Ives; God's Providence has placed you and Diana in our lives.

Thanks also to Paul Young, Brian and Becky Webb, Shirley Mullen, Ron Mahurin, Wayne MacBeth, and the students and staff at Houghton College. May the Lord bestow continued grace on Ellsworth Kalas, Leslie Andrews, Tom Tumblin, and all the men and women of God at Asbury Seminary. I am grateful to Rob Bell for lending me his round pulpit and humbled by the many pastors across the country who trust me with their flocks.

Heather and Ryan Bennett—may God continue to love others through you. Dan Dunn—you are a prince and a wicked good racquetball player. Jeff Rogers—your prayers are beautiful. Blessings to the Burnett, Bathje, Reynolds, Adams, Samson, Dunn, Ybarrola, Barker, Dixon, Robertson, Stratford, and Strawhun families for sustaining me with prayer, food, and fun.

Lastly, I love you, Clark, Emma, and Nancy. You are my better three-quarters and my greatest blessing on this earth.

Scripture Index

Old Testament

GENESIS
1:1-2, **22**
1:11-12, **138**
1:20, **29**
2:2-3, **81**
2:2, **72**
2:3, **73**
2:8-9, 15, **1**
2:8-15, **5**
2:8, **3**
2:15, **2**, **3**, **6**
2:16-17, **141**
2:18-22, **10**
3:17, **4**
3:19, **7**
4:12, **5**
6-9, **25**
6:5-6; 7:1-5, **21**
6:6, **25**
6:7, **6**
8:15-19; 9:13-15, **27**
15:5-6, **48**
17-18, **42**
17:7-8, **48**
18:1-8, **41**
19, **51**
21:33, **49**
22:1, **50**
40:18-22, **79**
41:1-8, **57**
41:33-36, **63**
49:5-7, **77**

EXODUS
2, **25**
3:14, **108**
7-10, **25**
9:29, **142**
14, **25**
15:1, **122**
16:22-30, **71**
17, **25**
20:8-11, **80**
23:19, **144**

LEVITICUS
18:26, 28, **63**
19:9-10, **95**
25:4-7, **143**
26, **6**

NUMBERS, 21:17, **122**

DEUTERONOMY
10:18-19, **43**
11:13-17, **6**
14:22-23, **141**
20:19, **61**
22:6-7, **60**
22, **143**
23:24-25, **94**
24:19, **95**
25:4, **143**
29, **142**
30:19-20, **65**

JOSHUA, 3, **25**

JUDGES, 5:24-27, **122**

RUTH
1:16-17, **93**
2:4-18, **88**

1 SAMUEL, 16:23, **122**

1 KINGS
17-18, **25**
17, **42**
18, **25**

2 KINGS, 6, **25**

1 CHRONICLES
15:28, **120**
29:11, **50**

2 CHRONICLES
7:6, **121**
7:13-14, **190**

JOB
5:9-10, **26**
12:7-10, **110**
12:10, **51**
29:16, **47**
38:7-11, **109**
38:18-38, **104**
38:25-27, **110**

PSALMS
19:1-2, **109**
19:1, **122**
23:1-6, **193**
24:1-2, **58**, **122**
24:1, **104**
24, **147**
31:15, **79**
33:2, **123**
36:8-9, **28**
42:1-2, **170**
46:10, **80**, **109**, **174**
57:8, **123**
65:9, **107**
65, 104, 107, **27**
71:22, **123**
72:1, 12-14, **97**
81:1-3, **124**
89:11, **148**
92:1-3, **126**
96:11-12, **108**
96:11-13, **122**
98:4, 7-9, **127**
104:10-13, **27**
104:24, **106**
104, **123-26**
133:1, **159**
147:4-5, **105**
147:7-9, **128**
148:3-6, **111**

148, **119**
149:1-5, **125**

PROVERBS
9:1-6, **11**
12:10, **143**
12:11, **9**
13:4, **9**
14:4, **9**
14:31, **91**
25:21, **140**
25:27, **141**
31:10-27, **9**
31:27, 26, **9**

ECCLESIASTES
2:24, **13**
3:1, **175**
5:12, **13**

SONG OF
  SOLOMON, **122**

ISAIAH
1:16-17, **28**
5:8-10, **62**
24:5-6, **189**
53:2-6, **188**
55:1-2, **145**
56:6-7, **75**
58:13-14, **78**

JEREMIAH
2:7, **143**
4:18, 20, **189**
22:3, **96**

EZEKIEL
20:20, **74**
34:18, **7**

DANIEL
1:8-15, **139**
1:8-16, **137**
1:11-16, **139**

MICAH
6:1-4, 7-8, **188**
6:1-4, **94**

New Testament

MATTHEW
1:5, **94**
5:1-2, **114**
5:42, **161**
5, **195**
6:9-10, **35**
6:25-26, **144**
6:25, **176**
11:28, **80**
12:1-2, **955**
13:24, **112**
13:31, **112**
14, **25**
22:37-40, **98**
25:34-35, **141**
25:34-45, **92**
25:35-36, **155**
25:35-46, **46**
25:35, **48**

MARK
2:27, **76, 81**
4:26, **112**
4, **25**

LUKE
1:46-55, **122**
3:7-12, **34**
5, **25**
6:31, **90**
11:2, **35**
14:13-14, **49**
16:19-26, **98**
22:19-20, **48**

JOHN
1:1-5, **30**
1:46, **191**

1:48, **191**
2, **25**
3:5, **24**
3:16, **188**
4:10-14, **28**
6:27, **8**
6:35, **189**
6:51, **146**
13:34, **88**
15:1, 5, **113**
15:1, **191**
21, **25**

ACTS
2:42-47, **153**
3:15, **190**
4:32-37, **157**
4:32, **158**
10:28, **146**

ROMANS
1:20, **29, 112**
3:9-10, **171**
5:17, **173**
8:6, **149**
8:19-23, **28**
8:22, **6, 188**
12:13, **45, 160**

1 CORINTHIANS
4:1-2, **59**
5:7, **53**
6:12, **177**
15:45, **190**

2 CORINTHIANS
5:14-15, **186**
5:17-18, **185**
11:24-27, **172**

EPHESIANS
4:28, **11**
5:1-5, **175**

PHILIPPIANS
2:3-4, **156, 167**
2:4-8, **93, 187**
4:4-9, **169**
4:8, **172, 178**
4:12-13, **178**

COLOSSIANS
1:13-23, **183**
1:15, **189**
1:19-20, **184**
2:20, **172**

1 TIMOTHY, 5:10,
  46

2 TIMOTHY, 1:7,
  179

HEBREWS
4:9-10, **77**
12:1, **176**
13:1-2, **53**
13:3, **175**

JAMES
1:27, **154**
2:26, **10**
4:17, **157**

1 PETER
4:9, **45**
5:4, **189**

1 JOHN, 4:7-8, **89**

REVELATION
5:5, **189, 190**
11:18, **14, 64**
22:16, **190**

Subject Index

abat (dress), 3

Abraham: binding of Isaac, testing of, 50; hospitality to the angels by, 41, 43; lineage and covenant made with, 47–48, 49; making God master of the house, 46; Targum on hospitality example using, 44–46; worthiness of, 49

Adam and Eve story, 7, 10–11, 25

addictions/cravings, 144, 148–49

agricultural laws: Christ's teachings on dietary and, 145–49; Old Testament, 141–43, 195–96

"All Creatures of Our God and King" (St. Francis of Assisi), 126–27

Ambrose of Milan, St., 16

animals: biblical dietary and agricultural laws on, 139–49, 195–96; compassion for, 27; flood story on Noah and the, 24–27

Annie's, 99

Anthony, St., 158, 159

Appalachia Mountains, 12

Arnold, Eberhard, 154

Ashley, 30, 31

At Blackwater Pond (Oliver), 34

Athanasius, St., 132

Augustine, 121

Austin's energy conservation power plant, 58–59

baptism, 34–35

Barnabas, 157

Barton, S. C., 53

Beecher, Henry Ward, 33, 84

Ben & Jerry's, 99

Berry, Wendell, 30

Bible: Abraham and the three angels, 41, 43; Adam and Eve story of the, 7, 10–11, 25; binding of Isaac story of the, 50; on community of God's people, 166; Daniel's story of the, 137–41, 149; examples of hospitality in the, 41, 42, 43, 44; flood story of the, 24–27; Job's story of the, 103–4, 107–9, 110, 113; psalms and music included in the, 120–23; Ruth's story of the, 87–88, 93–94. *See also* creation story; New Testament; Old Testament

biblical art, 193–94

Bildad, 108

binding of Isaac, 50

biracial population, 132

The Blue Zones (Buettner), 159

Boaz, 87–88, 95

Bob's Red Mill, 99

Boehme, Jacob, 14

Bonhoeffer, Dietrich, 173

Bruderhof (Platte Clove Community), 153–58, 166

Buechner, Frederick, 161

Buettner, Dan, 159

business recycling, 98–99

Calvin, John, 67

Canticle of the Sun (St. Francis of Assisi), 32

Cantico di fratre sole (Song of Brother Sun) [St. Francis of Assisi], 126–27

Caravaggio, Michelangelo, 193

Carver, George Washington, 116
Cascadian Farm, 99
chain restaurants, 163
change: longing for transformation
by God required for, 170; moving
toward simplicity, 170–79
Charlotte's Web (White), 174
Chernobyl nuclear accident, 58
Christ the Educator (St. Clement of
Alexandria), 68
Christian hospitality, 44, 49
The Church of the Eastern Christians
(Zernov), 193
Clean Water Act, 13
Clement of Alexandria, St., 68, 147, 148
Clinton, 82
clothes dryers, 12, 14, 15
coal energy: comparing nuclear and,
57–58; pollution and price of,
12–14, 58
Coleridge, Samuel Taylor, 82
Colorado River, 32
Columba, St., 133
commencement address, 184–85
Commentary on Genesis (Calvin), 67
Communality (Lexington), 164
communion, 50
community: Bible on God's people
and, 166; *Bruderhof* ("brotherhood") model of, 153–58, 166;
first-century church model of, 158;
home churches emergence in, 165;
hospitality to build, 160–61, 163;
improving the aesthetics of our,
163–64; modern challenges to living
in, 159–60; monastic model of, 158;
new monastic model of, 164; putting
needs of others first in, 156; sharing to build, 161, 162–63, 164; show
our love for God by reaching out to,
154–55; soul required for, 166; tolerance required for close, 165; virtual,
164; what you can do to encourage,
167–68. *See also* neighbors
compassion: for animals, 27; feeding the
hungry as form of, 142

*Compassion for Animals: Readings and
Prayers* (Linzey), 191
*The Complete Poetical Works of John
Greenleaf Whittier* (Whittier), 129
conservation: consequences of poor, 62;
energy, 12, 58–59, 69–70; as making biblical and common sense, 68;
politicized and polarizing topic of,
65; water, 32–33, 36–39. *See also*
environmental issues
consumerism: modern lifestyle of,
169–71; what you can do to combat,
180–81. *See also* simplicity
Contra Gentes (St. Athanasius), 132
Cornelius, 146
The Cosmic Christ (Maloney), 132
cravings/addictions, 144, 148–49
creation/nature: celebrating, 108; connection between Jesus and God's,
190; giving back sacrificially to
God's, 196, 197–98; God's creation
of, 58, 104; God's love for his creations and, 105; God's sacrifice
of his son to reconcile, 184; how
to celebrate, 117–18; intended to
sustain us, 107; learning from, 109;
learning humble attitude from, 110;
marveling at God's, 114–16; music to
care and celebrate, 119–33; organic
language origins in, 111–14; praising God's, 111; relationship between
God, earth and, 28; restoration
through relationship with, 189; trees,
4–5. *See also* earth
creation story: Adam and Eve story of,
7, 10–11, 25; association of water
with, 24, 25; doing work in harmony with, 9, 12; on God's seventh
day rest, 72, 73; of the waters and
the earth, 23; work as essential part
of, 3. *See also* Bible

"Dancing in the Streets" (Marvin Gaye),
129
Daniel's story, 137–41, 149
David, 122

da Vinci, Leonardo, 194
Day, Dorothy, 52, 165
day of rest: after completion of work, 10; creation story on God's seventh day, 72, 73, 81; as a gift, 76, 77, 78; how to celebrate your, 83–84; personal experience of keeping, 83–84; rewards of keeping, 75; "Stop days" as, 71–72, 73. *See also* work
desert father, 158
DeVito, Danny, 188
dietary laws: Christ's teachings on, 145–49; Daniel's story on following, 137–41, 149; how to encourage biblical practices of, 150–51
discontent, 177–78
The Division of Nature (Eriugena), 31
Donne, John, 158
doxology (glory words), 195–96
dress and keep, a garden commandment, 2–4
drinking water conservation: importance of, 32–33, 36–37; recommendations on ways to, 38–39

earth: creation of the waters and of, 23; defiling land through factory farming, 143–44; God's creation of the, 58, 104; God's promise to destroy the destroyers of, 14; poor stewardship and conservation practices impact on the, 62; relationship between God, creation and the, 28; resting the seventh year, 141–43. *See also* creation/nature; gardens
Earth Day, 195
Eden Foods, 99
electric clothes dryers, 12, 14, 15
Elijah, 42
Elijhu, 108
Eliphaz, 108
Elisha, 25
Elizabeth, 33
endangered species, 110
energy conservation: Austin's energy conservation power plant, 58–59; retrotechnology for, 12; ways that you can practice, 69–70
energy sources: coal, 12–14, 57–58, 58; nuclear, 57–58
environmental issues: learning from mistakes of the past, 66–67; politicized and polarizing nature of, 65; recycling, 97, 98–99. *See also* conservation; Tending the Garden
environmental music: to help in struggles faced by humanity, 130–33; how to celebrate God's gifts of, 134–35; psalms as, 121. *See also* music
Eriugena, John Scotus, 31
Ezra Taft Benson, Ensign (Beecher), 84

factory farming, 143–44
the Fall: Adam and Eve and, 7; work as not being punishment for, 3
"The Fall of Adam and the Decrees of God" (St. Symeon), 195
feeding the hungry, 141–42
flood story, 24–27
floppy baby (baby John Doe), 22–24
food: Christ's temptation of, 148, 149; Daniel's story on eating healthy, 137–41, 149; feeding the hungry, 141–42; as gift of God, 149; GMOs (genetically modified organisms), 147–48; God as the living bread, 146; how to encourage biblical practices related to, 150–51; provided by God to sustain humanity, 138; unhealthy habits of Americans related to, 140; vegetarian diet of, 141
food cravings, 144, 148–49
Francis of Assisi, St., 32, 126–27, 128
Frank, Anne, 75

Garbage Project (University of Arizona), 96
Garden of Eden: Adam and Eve's Fall in the, 7; day of rest kept in the, 81; job given to use in the, 17; trees planted in, 4

gardens: commandment to dress and keep a, 2–4; experience planting a family, 1–2; "God moments" experienced in, 6–7; suggestions for tending, 18–19. *See also* earth

Gaye, Marvin, 129–30

The Gleaners and I (documentary), 96

gleaning: Old Testament and New Testament on, 94–95; Panera restaurant practice of, 88–89; Sleeth family's experiment on, 96–97; stealing versus, 94; story of Ruth on, 87–88; story of 21st-century Ruth, 89–93. *See also* recycling

GMOs (genetically modified organisms), 147–48

God: covenant made with Abraham, 47–48; covenant with mankind through Adam, 25; creation of the earth by, 58, 104; dress and keep a garden commandment by, 2–4; hospitality making him master of the house, 46; hospitality to mankind by, 52–53; how to pray to, 35; as the living waters, 145; longing for transformation by, 170; made in image of, 4; Pascal on probability of existence of infinite, 67; praising, 125–33, 195–96; promise to destroy the destroyers of the earth, 14; relationship between earth, creation and, 28; sacrifice of his only son by, 184, 192; seventh day rest by, 72, 73, 81; testing of Abraham by, 50; trees as gift from, 5; water as symbol of, 28. *See also* Jesus Christ

God (Elihu), 108

"God moments," 6–7

God's love: for his creations, 105; reaching out to community as expression of, 154–55. *See also* love

Go Green, Save Green: A Simple Guide to Saving Time, Money and God's Green Earth (Sleeth), 19, 39, 55, 70, 86, 101, 118, 135, 151, 168, 181, 198

"Good Shepherd," 27, 189

Graham, Billy, 66

gratitude, 123, 128

The Great Divorce (Lewis), 166

Gregory Nazianzus, St., 191

Hagar, 47

Hammock Times (hypothetical magazine), 10

health/longevity factors, 159

home churches, 165

hospice care, 44

hospitality: by Abraham to the angels, 41, 43, 44–46; building community through, 160–61, 163; Christian, 44, 49; focus on family, friends, and strangers, 49; God's, 46, 52–53; of God to mankind, 52–53; Jesus' identification with, 48; Paul's words on, 45, 160; sacrifice connection to, 50–51; stewardship connection to, 43–44, 47; Targum to teach about, 44–46; what you can do to show, 54–55; of widow of Zarephath to Elijah, 42

humanity: as not the center of everything, 111; covenant between God, Adam and, 25; God's hospitality to, 52–53; learning humble attitude, 110; made in the image of God, 4; music for coping with struggles facing by, 130; variety of foods provided to sustain, 138

humbleness: developing attitude of, 110; earth is defiled for lack of, 189; as healing the land, 190; as sacrifice asked of God, 188

hyperconsumerism, 170

interracial marriage, 131

Irenaeus, 115

Isaac, 47, 49, 50

Israelites: agricultural laws given to, 141–43, 145–49, 195–96; dietary laws given to, 137–41, 145–51; led out of Egypt, 78–79; Sabbath Day instruction given to, 71, 80; Ten Commandments given to, 80

James, 146

Jesus Christ: artistic portrayals of, 193–94; connection with God's creation, 190; gleaning by disciplines and, 95; as the "Good Shepherd," 27, 189; identification with hospitality by, 48; Isaiah's prophetic description of, 187–88; John the Baptist's meeting and baptism of, 33–35; mastering the waters, 36; maternal lineage through Ruth to, 94; New Testament on story of, 29; organic language used by, 112–14; Paul on being imitators of, 175; as sacrifice, 184, 192; tempted by food, 148, 149; as tender root metaphor for, 187–91; various names of, 31; as the Word, 30. *See also* God; parables

"Jesus Loves the Little Children" (children's song), 131

Job's story, 103–4, 107–9, 110, 113

John the Baptist, 33–35

John Paul II, Pope, 29, 99, 166, 192

Joseph (Barnabas), 157

Joseph of Egypt, 59–64, 65

Journal (Wiberforce), 81

Julian of Norwich, 17

Kagan, Israel Meir ha-Kohen, 162

King Arthur, 99

Laban, 27

labor-saving devices: counterproductive consequences of, 11–17; description and use of, 8–9; Eve's "apple" as first, 7; slaves as, 9. *See also* work

Lent, 173

Lenten Message (1993) [John Paul II speech], 29

Levi, 77

Lewis, C. S., 166

lifestyle: consumerism, 169–71, 180–81; simplicity as, 170–79; 24/7, 75, 79, 82

Life Thoughts Gathered from the Extemporaneous Discourses of Henry Ward Beecher (Beecher), 33

Lincoln, Abraham, 83

Linzey, Andrew, 191

longevity factors, 159

Lord's Prayer, 35

love: community as solution for loneliness and, 165; reaching out to community as expression of, 154–55. *See also* God's love

Luke, 148

Luther, Martin, 15, 191

McDonough, William, 26

Magnificat (Luke 1:46–55), 122

Maloney, George, 132

Manual of Style (Strunk and White), 174

Marvelettes, 129

Mary, mother of Jesus, 33, 122

Meditation in the Spring Rain (Berry), 30

"Mercy, Mercy Me (The Ecology)" (Marvin Gaye), 129

Merton, Thomas, 28

Messiah (Handel), 188

Midrash Tanchuma, Kodashim 8, 164

Milton, 154, 156

miracles-water association, 25

Missionaries of Charity, 184–85

Modern Painters V (Ruskin), 13

monastic movement, 158

Moses: biblical story of, 25; birth and early life of, 75–76; on humane treatment of animals, 27; leads the Israelites out of Egypt, 78–79; Ten Commandments brought down by, 80

Muir, John, 131

music: awakening the spirit through, 123; of the Bible, 120–23; caring for God's creation through, 119–21; celebrating Lord's blessings with, 121, 124; for connecting with transcendence of God, 122–23; as echo of creation's beauty, 127; God's Word received with, 120; how to celebrate God's gifts of, 134–35; as joyful praise, 125–26; Magnificat (Luke 1:46–55) sung by Mary, 122; Marvin

Gaye's, 129–30. *See also* environmental music
My First Summer in the Sierras (Muir), 131
"My sweet Lord, my sweet Lord" (Marvin Gaye), 130

Naomi: biblical version of, 87–88, 89; modern version of, 90
Narnia, 6
Nathanael, 191
nature. *See* creation/nature
Nebuchadnezzar, 138
neighbors: helping your, 186; serving the interests of others and, 187; sharing with, 161, 162–63, 164. *See also* community
Newman's Own, 99
new monastic movement, 164
New Testament: on community of God's people, 166; on Jesus Christ of Nazareth, 29; on practice of gleaning, 94–95. *See also* Bible; Old Testament
New Yorker, 174
Noah, 24, 25, 26, 27
nuclear energy, 57–58

Old Testament: agricultural laws of, 141–43, 145–49, 195–96; on community of God's people, 166; dietary laws of the, 139–41, 145–51; on practice of gleaning, 94–95; on re-creation of the world, 29. *See also* Bible; New Testament
Oliver, Mary, 34
One Man's Meat (White), 174
organic language, 112–14

parables: organic language used in, 112; rich man and Lazarus, 97–98. *See also* Jesus Christ
Paradise (St. Ambrose of Milan), 16
Pascal, Blaise, 67
Pascal's Gambit (or Pascal's Wager) [Pascal], 67
Patrick, St., 9, 10

Paul: advocation of simplicity, 172, 173, 176, 177–78; on being imitators of Christ, 175; on building community, 160, 165; on hospitality to strangers, 45, 160; understanding God's nature, 29
"Peace with God, Peace with Creation" (John Paul II), 192
Pensees (Pascal), 67
Peter, 145–46, 165
Pharaoh of Egypt: Joseph and stewardship dream of, 57, 60–64, 65; of Moses' story, 25, 75–76, 78–79
Planet Earth (documentary), 176
Platte Clove Community (*Bruderhof*), 153–58, 166
"Please Mr. Postman" (Marvelettes), 129
pollution: coal mining production of, 13; retrotechnology to limit, 12
poverty: feeding the hungry and those in, 141–42; lack of trees as sign of, 5
praising God: doxology (glory words) for, 195–96; for his creation, 111; music for, 125–33
prayer, 35
Primitive Physic: or, An Easy and Natural Method of Curing Most Diseases (Wesley), 16

radio media, 174–75
Raids on the Unspeakable (Merton), 28
Ramses (Pharaoh of Egypt), 75, 76
Randy, 119–20
Rebecca, 27
recycling: as imperfect solution to disposal, 97; support of businesses engaged in, 98–99; toxic issue of, 98. *See also* gleaning
Red Sea mass drowning, 79
rest. *See* day of rest
The Resurrected Lord Appears to Mary Magdalene (Buckingham Palace), 190
retro technology, 12
rich man and Lazarus parable, 97–98
Ruskin, John, 13

Ruth's story: biblical version of, 87–88,
    93–94; modern version of, 89–93

Sabbath Day: as connecting God and
    humankind, 74; creation story on
    God's seventh day rest, 72, 73, 81;
    Exodus instructions on keeping
    the, 71; as a gift, 76, 77, 78; how to
    celebrate your day of rest, 85–86;
    personal experience of keeping the,
    83–84; resting the earth every sev-
    enth year, 141–43; rewards of keep-
    ing the, 75; Ten Commandments
    instruction on, 80. *See also* "Stop
    days"
sacrament, 121
sacrifice: to act justly and live humbly,
    188; binding of Isaac, 50; as Chris-
    tian faith foundation, 50; as element
    of simplicity, 172–73, 175; of God's
    son, 184, 192; hospitality connec-
    tion to, 50–51; of our pride, 190;
    self-interest versus, 185–86; of USS
    Dorchester's chaplains, 158; what you
    can do to sacrificially care for cre-
    ation, 197–98
Sarah: hospitality shown by Abraham
    and, 41, 42, 44, 45, 46; told she will
    conceive, 47, 49
Saul, 122
Schweitzer, Albert, 194
Seeds of Change, 99
segregation, 131–32
self-interest, 185–86
Serve God, Save the Planet (Sleeth), 73
Shabbat Shalam, 73, 81, 83
sharing: building community through,
    161, 162–63, 164; with the poor,
    100–101
shimar (keep), 3
Showings (Julian of Norwich), 17
Simeon, 77
simplicity: abstaining element of, 173–74;
    biblical counsel on, 170–72; journey
    toward practicing, 178–79; Paul's
    advocation of, 172, 173, 176, 177–78;

sacrifice as element of, 172–73, 175;
    television as distraction from, 174–75,
    177. *See also* consumerism
The Sin of Adam (St. Symeon), 195
Slate, Lester K., 104–7
Slate, Melody, 104, 106–7
Sleeth, Clark, 72
Sleeth, Emma, 52, 72, 88
Sleeth family: dietary practices followed
    by, 147; family garden experience of,
    1–2; gleaning experiment conducted
    by, 96–97; hospitality shown by,
    51–52; water conservation practices
    by, 31–32
Sleeth, J. Matthew: "stop days" practice
    of, 71–72, 73; youth-workers confer-
    ence attendance by, 88–89
Sleeth, Nancy: English essay written
    by student of, 82; family gardening
    started by, 6; *Go Green, Save Green:*
    by, 19, 39, 55, 70, 101, 118, 135, 151,
    168, 181, 198; hanging clothes to dry
    with, 14; hospitality shown by family
    and, 51–52, 160–61; speech given at
    college graduation of, 184; "stop day"
    activities with family and, 72; youth-
    workers conference attendance by,
    88–89
Sodom and Gomorrah, 51
Sollicitudo Rei Socialis (Papal Encyclical)
    [John Paul II], 99
Songs of Columba (St. Columba), 133
stealing, 94
Steve, 161
stewardship: consequences of poor, 62;
    hospitality connection to, 43–44, 47;
    Joseph of Egypt's story on, 59–64, 65;
    Pharaoh's dream on, 57, 60–64, 65
Stonyfield Farm, 99
"Stop days," 71–72, 73. *See also* Sabbath
    Day
Strunk, William, Jr., 174
Stuart Little (White), 174
suffering: Job's story on, 103–4, 107–9,
    110; Lester's story on, 104–7
Symeon the New Theologian, St., 195

Targum (hospitality), 44–46
television, 174–75, 177
Ten Commandments, 80
Tending the Garden: how to be intentionally green, 18–19; how to celebrate creation, 117–18; how to celebrate God's gifts of music and arts, 134–35; how to celebrate your day of rest, 85–86; how to conserve energy, 69–70; how to conserve water, 38–39; how to encourage biblical food practices, 150–51; how to show hospitality, 54–55; how you can share with the poor, 100–101; what you can do to combat consumerism, 180–81; what you can do to encourage community, 167–68; what you can do to sacrificially care for creation, 197–98. *See also* environmental issues
Teresa, Mother, 163, 173, 184–85, 196
thanksgiving, 123, 128
Three Mile Island nuclear accident, 58
tobacco, 173–74
tolerance, 165
trees: biblical role of, 4–5; Garden of Eden planting of, 4; as gift from God, 5
truth, 187
Tutu, Archbishop Desmond, 160
24/7 lifestyle, 75, 79, 82

University of Arizona's Garbage Project, 96
"Up, Up My Friend" (Wordsworth), 130
USS *Dorchester,* 196

vegetarian diet, 141
Vineyard Central Community, 164
virtual communities, 164

water conservation: how to practice, 38–39; importance of practicing, 31–33, 36–37
waters: being better stewards of life-giving, 28; creation association with, 24, 25; flood story association with, 24–27; Jesus' mastering of the, 36; miracles associated with, 25; power over living creatures, 29; as symbol of God, 28
The Way to Christ (Boehme), 14
Wendell (the cow), 147
Wesley, Charles, 15
Wesley, John, 15–16
What's Going On (Marvin Gaye), 129
White, E. B., 174–75
Whittier, John Greenleaf, 129
widow of Zarephath, 42
Wilberforce, William, 81
Winged Migration (documentary), 176
Woolman, John, 149
Wordsworth, William, 130
work: best work versus honest labor, 7–8; destructive versus constructive, 8; done in harmony with creation, 9, 12; as essential part of creation, 3; taking rest after completion of, 10; tending the garden commandment for, 6. *See also* day of rest; labor-saving devices
Works (Erlanger edition) [Luther], 15
The World of Albert Schweitzer (Schweitzer), 194

Zacchaeus, 191
Zernov, Nicholas, 193
Zophar, 108

THE GREEN BIBLE IS NOW AVAILABLE IN HARDCOVER AND PAPERBACK

Understand the Bible's Powerful Message for the Earth

Other Creation Care Resources from the Sleeth Family

BLESSED EARTH: HOPE FOR CREATION (DVD)
Matthew Sleeth, MD (Zondervan)

BLESSED EARTH: HOPE FOR HUMANITY (DVD)
Matthew Sleeth, MD (Zondervan)

DVD
curriculum

SERVE GOD, SAVE THE PLANET
Matthew Sleeth, MD (Zondervan)

GO GREEN, SAVE GREEN
Nancy Sleeth (Tyndale House)

IT'S EASY BEING GREEN
Emma Sleeth (Zondervan/Youth)

Available wherever books are sold

HarperOne
An Imprint of HarperCollinsPublishers